WORD POWER

in

15 Minutes a Day

LEARNINGEXPRESS ®

NEW YORK

Library of Congress Cataloging-in-Publication Data:
Junior skill builders : word power in 15 minutes a day.—1st ed.
    p. cm.
  ISBN: 978-1-57685-674-1
  1. Vocabulary—Study and teaching (Secondary)—Juvenile literature.   I. LearningExpress (Organization)
LB1631.J875 2009
428.1071'2—dc22   2008045364

Printed in the United States of America

10 9 8 7 6 5 4 3 2 1

First Edition

For more information or to place an order, contact LearningExpress at:
  2 Rector Street
  26th Floor
  New York, NY 10006

Or visit us at:
  www.learnatest.com

C O N T E N T S

⒤ ⒩ ⒯ ⒭ ⓞ ⒟ ⒰ ⒞ ⒯ ⒤ ⓞ ⒩

CONGRATULATIONS ON YOUR DECISION to increase your word power. The definition of word power is *having a strong vocabulary*. That doesn't mean just knowing lots of words; it means being able to use them comfortably and effectively.

Building word power may be one of the most important tasks you accomplish in your school years—apart from graduation itself, of course! Writing school assignments is usually a big challenge, and what single thing could make writing easier? The answer is simple: knowing enough of the right words to say what you mean so you can finish the writing assignment.

Having a good vocabulary is valuable outside of school as well. Having just the right words in your mind, or at the tip of your tongue, lets you express your thoughts precisely. We've all experienced the frustration of knowing what we mean, but not being able to communicate our thoughts to others. That frustration is usually linked to vocabulary, because *the more words you know, the easier it is to communicate your ideas*. And the ability to communicate is necessary all through your life, not just in your school years. With lots of useful words in your vocabulary, you'll send more interesting IMs and text messages to friends, write wonderful thank you notes to relatives, and get a better job (and keep it) when you start working!

This book is designed to help you build word power in an easy, efficient way. *If you invest just 15 minutes a day with this book, you'll increase your word power dramatically.* You will have acquired hundreds of new words to use at school, at home, with friends, and anywhere else for the rest of your life!

Here's how it works: The book is divided into 30 lessons. Each lesson requires you to spend just 15 minutes learning new words and doing simple exercises to cement those words in your vocabulary. So your word power increases every day, and, if you keep on schedule, you'll have added several new words to your vocabulary by the end of the month!

Time to get started. Today is the first day of your vocabulary power-up. You'll find that building word muscle isn't such hard work—and it can actually be lots of fun!

HOW THIS BOOK WILL INCREASE YOUR WORD POWER

Think of this book as a vocabulary savings bank: with each lesson, you add to your word power and get richer. And as you do this, you earn interest on your investment for the future. Once you learn a word, you almost never forget it. It gets filed in your word bank account—your brain—and is available for you to use the rest of your life!

The book is divided into four sections designed to build word power in various ways. Each of the 30 lessons focuses on a specific vocabulary skill or family of words.

Section 1: Tools for Building Word Power. In these first nine lessons, you'll review word roots and common prefixes and suffixes (word beginnings and endings), and gain tricks and techniques for learning new words.

Section 2: Use Different Parts of Speech to Increase Word Power. These lessons help you build an inventory of useful nouns, verbs, adjectives, and adverbs to make your writing and speaking more powerful.

Section 3: Build Word Power in All Subject Areas. Think of a part of your life that interests you, and find ways to increase your word power on the subject.

Section 4: Build Word Power in Special Ways. The final section of the book covers ways to use slang, foreign phrases, and confusing and extra fancy words to beef up your vocabulary and become an extremely powerful wordsmith.

The book uses carefully designed features to make learning quick and easy:

- Truly useful, versatile words that you'll find yourself using right away. No lists of longest/hardest/rarest words are included. The words here give you real word power, not silly tricks.
- Basic, simple definitions of new words. No long, complicated historical references, just the meaning you need to use a word correctly.
- Samples of new words in useful, believable sentences. Sample sentences are like those you might hear or say in normal conversation.
- Easy-to-understand phonetic pronunciation guides, in cases where it may be tough to figure out how to say an unknown word.
- A variety of exercises to keep you interested and challenged, and help you get the new words filed permanently in your memory bank.
- Tips and techniques for figuring out the meanings of new words you hear or read.
- Dictionary, thesaurus, and other resources (some online) that can help you build word power as you work with this book and after.
- A list at the end of each lesson: *Words You Should Now Know*. These are words defined and/or used in the lesson that may be new to you. If a word has not been defined in the lesson, and you don't recognize it, use a dictionary to look it up.
- A list of *Extra Word(s) You Learned in This Lesson*. This feature provides space for you to record additional new word(s) you may have learned in the lesson.

You'll get the most out of this book if you do the lessons in Section 1 in order, because each lesson builds on skills from earlier lessons. But once you've finished the first section, feel free to do the rest of the lessons in a different order. What's important is that you complete *all* the lessons, and review any that seemed tricky the first time. If you stick with the plan, in just one month you'll have word power to brag about!

Your book also includes a pretest and a posttest to help you evaluate word power before and after using the lessons. On the pretest, you're not expected to get all the answers right. If you did, you wouldn't need this book!

The difference in your two scores after you take the posttest will show you how your word power has increased!

Each lesson takes just 15 minutes. If you'll invest that very small amount of time each day to read and absorb a lesson's material and answer a few questions, you'll noticeably improve your vocabulary. Now, doesn't that sound workable?

TIP: The Best Way to Improve Your Vocabulary and Build Word Power

The single most effective way to improve your vocabulary is simply this: READ! If you read at least 15 minutes a day, every day, your vocabulary will certainly improve. And it doesn't really matter what you read; even comics are fine. So read—anything. Books. Newspapers. Magazines. Internet sites. Without realizing it, you'll learn new vocabulary words, new sentence structures, new information—and, of course, you'll be building your word power!

P R E T E S T

THIS PRETEST HAS 30 questions that test your knowledge of the kinds of vocabulary skills covered in this book. The test should take about 30 minutes to complete, and will provide a sense of your existing vocabulary knowledge.

The answer key is at the end of the test. It also includes the lesson number in which each question's vocabulary word appears. Don't peek and good luck!

1. An *advocate* is
   a. a criminal lawyer.
   b. a member of the legislature.
   c. a kind of tropical fruit.
   d. someone who speaks for an idea or a person.

2. The word *context* means the

   a. surrounding or background of something.

   b. list of contents in a book.

   c. index at the back of a book.

   d. best way to complete a sentence.

3. When you call something *explicit,* you mean it

   a. is very complicated.

   b. is very simple.

   c. is clearly stated.

   d. cannot be easily understood.

4. The *root* of a word is the

   a. ending of a word.

   b. main part of a word.

   c. beginning of a word.

   d. origin of a word.

5. A *prefix* is the

   a. syllable at the beginning of a word.

   b. syllable at the end of a word.

   c. place where a word begins.

   d. idea that is the word's starting point.

6. The word *stationery* describes

   a. something that doesn't move.

   b. a statue in a public park.

   c. writing paper and envelopes.

   d. a service place, such as a gas station.

7. The word *dessert* describes

   a. a dry landscape with cactus and no grass.

   b. the tropical part of a jungle.

   c. the ending of a story.

   d. the sweet part served at the end of a meal.

8. The word *duel* describes
   a. something that is double.
   b. having two or more of an item.
   c. a formal fight between opponents.
   d. the second place winner in a race.

9. To *persecute* someone is to
   a. try them for a crime.
   b. count them as part of a group.
   c. find someone guilty of a crime.
   d. punish or pursue in an extreme manner.

10. A *hostel* is
   a. a place where animals live.
   b. a fairly inexpensive hotel.
   c. a hostess at a company party.
   d. an introduction to a play.

11. *Adjectives* are words that
   a. convey the action in a sentence.
   b. describe or modify nouns in a sentence.
   c. act as helpers to the verb in a sentence.
   d. determine when the action is happening.

12. The word *inherent* means
   a. a natural part of something that cannot be separated.
   b. an extra part of something that can easily be separated.
   c. the last item in a list or series.
   d. something that can be divided into at least two parts.

13. The word *predominant* refers to the
   a. least important part of a subject.
   b. opening paragraph in an essay or short story.
   c. final explanation in an essay or short story.
   d. most common or important part of something.

14. To do something *frantically* means
   a. to do it with great care.
   b. to do it with great energy.
   c. to do it in a rush or a panic.
   d. to do it with a lot of style and attitude.

15. To do something *vigorously* means
   a. to do it with great energy and strength.
   b. to do it with a lot of style and attitude.
   c. to do it with great care and caution.
   d. to do it in a rush or a panic.

16. Someone who is *altruistic* is
   a. a person who has great wealth.
   b. a person who is selfish and self-involved.
   c. a person who cares unselfishly for others.
   d. a person who is always honest.

17. A *gourmet* is someone who
   a. knows a lot about the subject of food.
   b. knows a lot about the subject of literature.
   c. knows a lot about the subject of finance.
   d. knows a lot about the subject of fashion.

18. A *narcissist* is
   a. a person who cares about style.
   b. a person who always thinks about money.
   c. a person who thinks only of him- or herself.
   d. a person who is ambitious politically.

19. To have *contempt* for people is to
   a. care about their welfare.
   b. consider them not worthy of respect.
   c. consider them very important.
   d. be jealous of them.

20. If you are *gluttonous*, you are
    a. a good team player.
    b. an accomplished athlete.
    c. willing to try anything.
    d. someone who eats a lot.

21. If you are having trouble hearing, you should go to
    a. a dermatologist.
    b. an audiologist.
    c. an internist.
    d. an ophthalmologist.

22. The doctor who helps straighten teeth is
    a. an optometrist.
    b. an audiologist.
    c. an orthodontist.
    d. a dermatologist.

23. *Aerobic* exercise is
    a. working out with free weights.
    b. running at least a mile a day.
    c. exercise that builds muscles.
    d. exercise in which the heart pumps faster and the body uses more oxygen.

24. *Calisthenics* are exercises that
    a. require the use of free weights.
    b. require the use of no equipment.
    c. require a great deal of cross training.
    d. require large muscle mass.

25. *Kinetic* is a word that describes
    a. something that is produced by motion.
    b. something that is stationary and never moves.
    c. something that builds muscle strength.
    d. something that builds stamina.

26. To *facilitate* is to
   a. state the same idea twice.
   b. find something useful to contribute.
   c. offer an opposing argument.
   d. make something happen easily.

27. *Hierarchy* is a word that describes
   a. a group with power.
   b. a democratic committee.
   c. an arrangement by rank or importance.
   d. a set of ideas or beliefs.

28. A *faux pas* is
   a. a mistake in manners or conduct.
   b. an instrument of torture.
   c. a last chance to save someone.
   d. a damage to someone's reputation.

29. A *matinee* is
   a. a matter of politics.
   b. an elegant French dessert.
   c. a computer video program.
   d. an afternoon performance.

30. A *pirouette* is
   a. the topping on a pie.
   b. the point of a fountain pen.
   c. a ballet step.
   d. a French candy.

ANSWERS

1. **d** (Lesson 3)
2. **a** (Lesson 3)
3. **c** (Lesson 3)
4. **b** (Lesson 5)
5. **a** (Lesson 5)
6. **c** (Lesson 7)
7. **d** (Lesson 7)
8. **c** (Lesson 9)
9. **d** (Lesson 9)
10. **b** (Lesson 10)
11. **b** (Lesson 11)
12. **a** (Lesson 11)
13. **d** (Lesson 11)
14. **c** (Lesson 13)
15. **a** (Lesson 13)
16. **c** (Lesson 14)
17. **a** (Lesson 14)
18. **c** (Lesson 14)
19. **b** (Lesson 16)
20. **d** (Lesson 16)
21. **b** (Lesson 19)
22. **c** (Lesson 19)
23. **d** (Lesson 23)
24. **b** (Lesson 23)
25. **a** (Lesson 23)
26. **d** (Lesson 24)
27. **c** (Lesson 24)
28. **a** (Lesson 26)
29. **d** (Lesson 26)
30. **c** (Lesson 26)

SECTION 1

tools for building word power

MEMORIZING LISTS OF new words is boring and definitely no fun. And actually, memorizing is not an efficient way to increase your word inventory—the memorized words are quickly forgotten. In the first nine lessons of this book, you'll review (or learn for the first time) how to use some language basics, such as knowledge of word roots, common prefixes and suffixes (word beginnings and endings), and additional tricks and techniques, to help you learn new words and remember them.

1

why work on your vocabulary?

Words are a lens to focus one's mind.
—AYN RAND (1905–1982)
AMERICAN NOVELIST AND PHILOSOPHER

This lesson reviews five important reasons to improve your vocabulary, and gives you some short diagnostic test questions to help you evaluate your word power strengths and weaknesses.

VOCABULARY LISTS? UGH. Word tests? Double ugh. Spelling tests? Triple, triple ugh.

Sound familiar? Many people have uttered those *ughs*, silently or out loud—and probably more than once. At first glance, studying words and their meanings (and their correct spellings) may not appear to be a fun activity, but few areas of study can bring you more rewards in the long run.

Here are some important reasons to increase your word power.

1. **You'll do better on tests**—and not just vocabulary tests. Knowing more words is the key to showing your teachers that you've been reading your assignments and absorbing the ideas you're taught. You'll have an impressive inventory of words to choose from when answering questions.
2. **Your thought process will improve.** One problem you might have run into when writing an essay is that it requires a certain word count, but you can't think of enough to write about! When

your vocabulary knowledge increases, you can describe your ideas, feelings, opinions, and facts more precisely because you have more words at your disposal. Before you know it, you'll not only write thoughtful, descriptive essays—you'll meet that word count and have more to say than ever before!

3. **You'll better understand the things you read.** You get most of the new information you learn, in school and out in the world, by reading. Think of all the reading you do: on websites and blogs you visit, sending and receiving text messages, listening to songs. Commercials, television shows, and movies you see are full of words. Every medium, whether it's something you're assigned in school or something you've chosen to experience as entertainment, is at least partly made up of words. The more words you know, the more you'll be able to understand and appreciate new things.

4. **You'll impress people** with your word power. This may seem like a superficial reason to build vocabulary, but think about it. Right now, you're a student and you want to impress your teachers and prove your academic abilities to them. Once you're out in the working world, you'll find it's even more important to make a good impression—on future bosses, for example. And both now and in the future, you've got to convince friends and family that you know what you're talking about and you mean what you say.

What better way to accomplish these goals than to have an extensive inventory of words! That's what impressing people is all about: making a good impression because you've found the words to say exactly what you mean.

Can you think of any other reasons to build your word power? If so, jot them down here:

Even More Reasons to Build Word Power

_____

_____

_____

_____

MEASURING YOUR WORD POWER STRENGTHS AND WEAKNESSES

The pretest you took before starting this section gave you a general evaluation of your word power skills. You may wish that you'd scored higher on that test, but never fear. You're on your way to improving your word power by reading and completing the lessons in this book. After those, you'll ace the posttest!

PRACTICE: FINDING OUT WHAT YOU ALREADY KNOW

The following three diagnostic questions will help you spot specific areas you need to concentrate on to have greater word power. There are no right or wrong answers; just try to complete the questions quickly and easily.

1. **Vocabulary Fluency: What Does That Word Mean?**
   This question tests your ability to use antonyms, or words with opposite meanings. If you know what a word means, you should be able to supply its opposite very easily.
   In the blank next to each word, write a word that means the opposite.
   Time: one minute

Test Word	An Opposite Word
sweet	
different	
asleep	
run	
easy	

Was this question easy for you? Did you zoom through it? If so, you don't seem to have problems with fluency—the ability to find the right word easily in your vocabulary inventory. If you hesitated, or were stumped and unable to think of an opposite word, you'll need to pay particular attention to remembering the meanings of new words you learn. Be sure to practice carefully, using new words in conversation or written sentences.

2. Using Synonyms: Do You Know Another Word?

Synonyms are words that have the same meaning. This question tests your ability to supply synonyms for sample words.

In the blank next to each word, write a word with a similar meaning. Remember, there may be more than one synonym. Write the first one that comes to your mind.

Time: one minute

Test Word	A Similar Word
strange	
rude	
correct	
enormous	
rule	

How did you do? This question tested your ability to use synonyms, or words with similar (if not exactly identical) meanings. If this question was a breeze for you, you can be somewhat confident about your ability to find synonyms in your vocabulary inventory. This skill is important to reading comprehension as well as to writing. If you hesitated, or found it difficult to think of a synonym, you'll need to pay particular attention to acquiring new words. Your vocabulary may be weak and in need of some strengthening.

3. Using the Right Homonym: Is That Word Spelled Correctly?

Homonyms are words that are pronounced the same way but have entirely different meanings.

Circle the correct word in each sentence.

Time: one minute.

1. Ethan dropped his subway token down the street (great/grate) and suddenly had no way to get home.
2. His day at the (beech/beach) had been loads of fun, but now he was really stuck.
3. Wondering what to do, Ethan scraped the (souls/soles) of his flip-flops along the curb nervously, waiting for inspiration to strike.
4. If he remained (stationery/stationary) and kept hoping, then maybe a friend would come along and lend him an extra token.
5. On the other hand, if he continued to (waist/waste) time standing still, he'd be in big trouble once he finally got home.

If you found these questions easy to answer, you're probably a fairly good speller. But you can't be too careful. Some of the most common test-taking and essay-writing errors occur when students rush through their work and fail to double check their spelling. If you had to think hard to answer any of these questions, you'll need to pay special attention to spelling, which is a skill often overlooked in word power.

SET YOUR WORD POWER LEARNING GOALS

Now that you've completed these brief practice exercises, you should have an idea of which areas of vocabulary improvement you need to concentrate on. Is it spelling? Is it understanding word meaning? Is it knowing words well enough to use them casually in conversation and writing?

In the space below, list the areas you want to improve, and remember, deciding to improve in more than one area is certainly allowed!

My Word Power Goals
1.
2.
3.

Lesson 1 Words You Should Now Know

antonym	inventory
diagnostic	stationary
enormous	stationery
fluency	synonym
homonym	

ANSWERS

Practice: Finding Out What You Already Know

1. **Vocabulary Fluency.** Possible antonyms (opposite words) include:
   sweet: sour, salty, bitter, spicy
   different: same, similar, alike
   asleep: awake, alert, waking, conscious
   run: walk, stumble, hop, stand still
   easy: difficult, hard, complicated
2. **Knowing Synonyms.** Possible synonyms (same or very similar words) include:
   strange: odd, weird, alien, uncommon, unusual
   rude: ill-behaved, ill-mannered, vulgar, inconsiderate, impolite
   correct: right, appropriate, true, valid
   enormous: large, gigantic, huge
   rule: nouns: law, principle, regulation; **verbs:** legislate, reign, govern, run
3. **Using the Correct Homonym**
   1. grate
   2. beach
   3. soles
   4. stationary
   5. waste

tools and techniques
for learning new words

The finest language is mostly made up
of simple unimposing words.
—GEORGE ELIOT (1819–1880)
PEN NAME OF MARY ANN EVANS, ENGLISH NOVELIST

This lesson introduces a variety of useful resources to help you improve your word power. You'll also learn vocabulary building techniques and tricks to help you in both written and spoken communication now and in the future.

LEARNING NEW WORDS isn't a magical process. And it's not rocket science. It just takes a willingness to learn and an appreciation of how useful words can be. It's important to remember that the best words aren't necessarily the longest ones—or the strangest ones. Indeed, most great writers agree that the best words are the simple ones that express thoughts in plain language that's sincere and direct.

All this means is that if you want to improve your word power and the ability to communicate effectively, you can. You'll just need some valuable resources and time-tested techniques to make words stick in your word bank.

TOOLS FOR BUILDING WORD POWER

A Good Ear

The very best tools for building vocabulary are attached to your head: your two ears! Listening carefully is an ideal way to pick up new words. If you concentrate on listening for new words, you'll discover that you hear them every day. You'd be amazed at how often new words whiz past you! (In Lesson 3, you'll learn to figure out a new word's meaning by noticing the other words in the sentence.)

TIP: Go back to the Introduction and reread the tip on ways to build word power. Remember, the most effective way is to read!

KEEP A PERSONAL WORD BOOK

When you read or hear an unfamiliar word, write it down so you can look it up later. Often, writing a word helps you commit it to memory. Some people are *visual learners*, who remember new things best when they see the written words or ideas. Other people are *auditory learners*, who remember things more easily if they're spoken or sung. Which kind of memory learner are you? Either way, it's a great idea to keep a daily notebook in which you write any new words you hear or see.

TIP: Challenge your best friend to keep a word book, too, and compare the books every few weeks, exchanging new words. Compete to see who gets the longest list. Loser treats winner to an after-school snack!

WORD SEARCH BOOKS AND CROSSWORD PUZZLES

If you take the bus or other public transportation, or spend time sitting around an airport, you probably see people with word search or crossword puzzle books. These activities are popular because they keep minds active while teaching new and interesting words. They also provide a challenging, fun way to pass the time.

If you haven't tried these kinds of puzzles, check your local newspaper or go online to look for them. Puzzle books are sold in most bookstores, so you may want one to keep in your backpack for down time. You may well become a real word puzzle fan, which could be a good thing. Who knows, you just might turn into a famous writer someday!

DICTIONARIES

This may seem obvious, or boring, but don't underestimate the value of a dictionary. You should make it a habit to use a dictionary in two ways.

1. Look up the meanings of words you don't know.
2. While looking up a word, note other words printed near it. Browse, and you may find some other, really fascinating ones you don't know on the same page!

WHICH DICTIONARY IS BEST?

Look around your home, and you'll probably find a dictionary sitting on a shelf somewhere. This can be an invaluable tool in building your vocabulary. A dictionary provides a lot of useful information about words: how to pronounce them, their grammatical functions, their history and development, and any multiple meanings of words. Most of the time, you won't use all this information, but its usefulness and overall value will increase with time. There will most likely come a day when you'll find yourself using a dictionary's detailed information more frequently.

ONLINE DICTIONARIES AND VOCABULARY TOOLS

If you spend time online, you should become familiar with all the dictionary help available on the Internet. Use the online resources by typing the word in the search box, or if you want to be more specific, type in definition + the word you want. You'll be offered definitions of that word from several dictionaries and encyclopedias. Typically, along with the definition, you'll find lists of or links to antonyms and synonyms from a thesaurus.

WORD OF THE DAY

Build your word power and help feed hungry people of the world at the same time—for free! It's a win-win situation! At www.freerice.com, you are given a word and four possible meanings. Click on the right meaning and you donate 20 grains of rice to the United Nations World Food Program. (You'll see the rice grains appear in a bowl.) If you get the answer wrong, you are told the right answer and given an easier word to define. After each right answer, you'll have the chance to define more words, including any you got wrong along the way, and watch the rice fill the bowl. You may have so much fun that you'll want to donate a bowl of rice each day!

TIP: Be very careful when searching in online dictionaries. These websites often include advertisements that try to pull you away from the academic definitions. While you may find the additional material interesting, it's not always accurate or true.

BEWARE OF THE THESAURUS

A thesaurus is a book that provides synonyms and antonyms for words. Use a thesaurus to look up a word and find many other words that have the same (or the opposite) meaning as that word. But be careful! Thesauruses don't explain the nuances, or subtle differences in meaning, that exist among words that seem to have the same or nearly the same meaning. For example, look at this short list of synonyms that a thesaurus provides for the word *adequate*:

competent, modest, sufficient, suitable, decent, equal

Now, imagine using any of these words in the following sentence:

Sally, the hardest-working student in our class, has a vocabulary that is _____.

Would each of these words create the same meaning if it were plugged into the sentence? Hardly. To say that Sally's vocabulary is *suitable* is very different from saying that it is *sufficient* or *adequate*. And saying it is *equal* doesn't make any sense at all.

Avoid using a thesaurus unless you know for sure that the word you've chosen conveys exactly the meaning you want. The thesaurus is a writing tool to use only after you have a very extensive vocabulary of your own. Then, you can choose from the words supplied with a better understanding of all their meanings.

WORD SEARCH—JUST FOR FUN!

Here's a word search utilizing ten words taken from this lesson. See how quickly you can find all of them, in the word search as well as in the previous pages.

PRACTICE: VOCABULARY BUILDING WORD SEARCH

Find and circle the words from this lesson hidden in the word search puzzle below. Words may appear backwards, vertically, or horizontally.

```
T  S  C  A  P  T  S  H  J  O  L  C  Y  U  L
M  E  I  H  L  L  C  Y  E  N  O  T  P  E  A
R  A  C  T  A  W  D  S  N  M  A  Q  F  G  C
S  C  O  H  T  L  S  I  M  O  N  G  B  V  I
R  E  D  D  N  J  L  U  A  M  N  E  S  W  G
F  I  S  H  E  I  N  E  C  X  Z  Y  M  N  A
A  P  R  I  G  I  C  H  N  Q  L  K  M  F  M
H  O  U  S  C  A  T  A  B  G  D  P  J  G  I
Q  R  A  A  V  B  X  I  L  P  E  E  S  O  T
Y  O  T  B  G  N  I  T  A  N  I  C  S  A  F
E  E  I  T  O  B  V  I  O  U  S  K  L  G  A
L  I  T  T  P  R  A  G  E  N  U  I  N  E  J
E  T  A  M  I  T  S  E  R  E  D  N  U  A  N
P  F  A  S  E  L  S  I  G  E  N  I  O  B  I
J  E  X  P  R  O  N  E  W  Q  T  O  N  R  N
```

Word Bank

challenge	ninja
communicate	obvious
fascinating	synonym
genuine	technical
magical	underestimate

Lesson 2 Words You Should Now Know

fascinating	obvious
genuine	technical
ninja	thesaurus
nuance	underestimate

Extra Word(s) You Learned in This Lesson

_____

_____

_____

_____

ANSWERS

Practice: Vocabulary Building Word Search

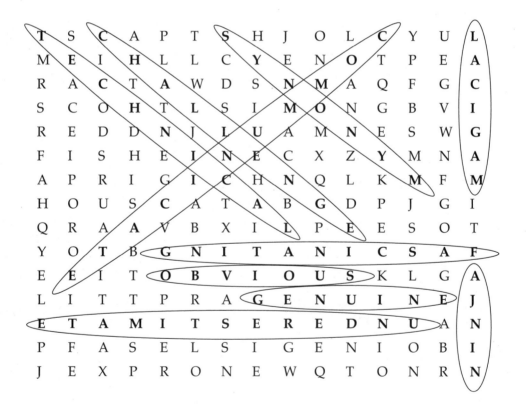

```
T  S  C  A  P  T  S  H  J  O  L  C  Y  U  L
M  E  I  H  L  L  C  Y  E  N  O  T  P  E  A
R  A  C  T  A  W  D  S  N  M  A  Q  F  G  C
S  C  O  H  T  L  S  I  M  O  N  G  B  V  I
R  E  D  D  N  J  L  U  A  M  N  E  S  W  G
F  I  S  H  E  I  N  E  C  X  Z  Y  M  N  A
A  P  R  I  G  I  C  H  N  Q  L  K  M  F  M
H  O  U  S  C  A  T  A  B  G  D  P  J  G  I
Q  R  A  A  V  B  X  I  L  P  E  E  S  O  T
Y  O  T  B  G  N  I  T  A  N  I  C  S  A  F
E  E  I  T  O  B  V  I  O  U  S  K  L  G  A
L  I  T  T  P  R  A  G  E  N  U  I  N  E  J
E  T  A  M  I  T  S  E  R  E  D  N  U  A  N
P  F  A  S  E  L  S  I  G  E  N  I  O  B  I
J  E  X  P  R  O  N  E  W  Q  T  O  N  R  N
```

use a word's context to figure out its meaning

"When I use a word," Humpty Dumpty said in
rather a scornful tone, "it means just what
I choose it to mean—neither more nor less."
—LEWIS CARROLL (1832–1898)
PEN NAME OF CHARLES LUTWIDGE DODGSON, ENGLISH AUTHOR

This lesson focuses on figuring out the meanings of new words from clues around them, and provides sample exercises to help you practice using this invaluable skill.

BEFORE YOU BEGIN this lesson, make sure you understand the meaning of *context*:

> **context** (noun):
> 1. the sentence in which a word appears that often helps the reader understand its meaning
> 2. the surroundings, circumstances, environment, background, or settings that determine, specify, or clarify the meaning of an event

Looking at the context in which an unfamiliar word appears may be an easy way to determine the word's meaning. You've been doing just that all your life without even thinking about it. When you were an infant and beginning to understand words, your parents taught you by using context. For example, your mother might have handed you a piece of apple and said, *apple.* So that's how you learned the word, by connecting it in context to a crunchy, juicy object you could eat!

Now, you're older and reading on your own, but you can use the same kinds of surrounding clues to determine the meanings of words new to you. Here's an example of how it works. What's the meaning of the underlined word in the following sentence?

Sherlock Holmes *deciphered* the mystery of the crook's identity by puzzling out the clues left behind at the scene of the crime.

    a. wrote
    b. forgot
    c. photographed
    d. discovered

If you chose *d*, you figured out the meaning of *decipher* by using other words in the sentence. Knowing that Sherlock Holmes was trying to solve a crime helped you eliminate words that didn't make sense, like *forgot*, *photographed*, and *wrote*. The words *puzzling out* probably helped you, too. And through a process of elimination, you figured out that in this sentence, *deciphered* means "discovered." Here's the dictionary definition of decipher:

decipher (verb): to make out the meaning of something that is difficult to read

Example: I cannot decipher his handwriting.

....

TIP: When you learn a new word, try to use it soon (and frequently) in everyday speech. Record the new word in your personal word book, and make a point of using it in the next day or so.

....

PRACTICE: DISCOVERING MEANING FROM CONTEXT

Circle *in pencil* (in case you change your mind) the choice you think is the correct definition of the italicized word. If you don't know the meaning of the word *italicized*, you should be able to figure it out from the context. An explanation of the correct answer follows each question, so read slowly and carefully—and don't peek ahead at the explanation!

1. Make sure you give your parents *explicit* directions for where to pick you up after soccer practice.
   a. complicated
   b. clearly stated
   c. in chronological order
   d. factual

You can eliminate *complicated* and *in chronological order* because they don't make sense. Why would you want to give complicated directions? That wouldn't help anyone get there to pick you up in time. And *chronological order* means putting things in sequence according to when they happened. This sentence is about something that will happen in the future. *Factual* also doesn't make sense because it suggests there are two kinds of directions—factual ones and imaginary ones! So, by a process of elimination, you should choose *clearly stated* as the meaning of *explicit*.

2. Although it was *futile*, Tom insisted on applying to become a member of the girls' soccer team, even though he knew he didn't meet the most basic requirement.
   a. useless
   b. fruitful
   c. possible
   d. likely

The context tells you that Tom doesn't meet the most basic requirement, so you can eliminate *possible* and *fruitful*, both of which suggest good, positive outcomes for his application. *Futile* means "useless," producing no result, like Tom's application.

3. Brittany considered her parents' rules an *enigma*; she couldn't understand why they wanted her to be home so early every afternoon.
   a. an enemy
   b. a solution
   c. a mystery
   d. a good idea

The second half of the sentence tells you Brittany doesn't understand the rules, so you can eliminate *an enemy* and *a good idea*. It's unlikely that she considers their rules *a solution*, so you should have chosen *a mystery*. An *enigma* is something that's puzzling or difficult to understand.

4. The principal is extremely popular with the students because he is a strong *advocate* of students' rights.

   a. opponent

   b. enemy

   c. member

   d. supporter

You might have picked *enemy* because some students don't like their principal, but the context of the sentence tells you that this principal is popular. So you can eliminate *opponent* as well. *Member* isn't logical; students and principals aren't usually members of the same group. *Supporter* is the right choice here. To be an *advocate* means to actively support an idea or a group.

5. One *component* of Tim's outfit was a baseball cap turned sideways on his head; another was his sagging pants.

   a. distraction

   b. color

   c. disappointment

   d. part

This is a difficult choice. The word *component* means one of several parts that make up a whole, usually a machine or a system. For example, earphones are a component of an iPod. So *part* is the best choice. But you might have chosen either *distraction* or *disappointment*, if any surrounding sentences seemed to criticize Tim's general appearance.

6. The decision to convert the school year to a ten-month calendar was very *controversial* among both students and teachers.

   a. creating popularity

   b. causing excitement

   c. creating profits

   d. causing disagreement

As a student, you probably found this choice fairly easy. You can eliminate *creating profit*, because it would be highly unlikely for changing the calendar to make money for the school. The fact that both students and teachers are involved here should help you choose either *a* or *d*. Choice *a* is a logical possibility; there may be students somewhere in the world who want a shorter summer, but have you ever met one? The correct choice is *d*. Something that's *controversial* causes disagreement; it's something about which people have different opinions.

7. Jennifer *implied* that she wanted to be Jim's girlfriend, but she didn't say so directly.
   a. hinted
   b. declared
   c. refused
   d. questioned

The context tells you that Jennifer has chosen not to say something directly, so the definition of the word *implied* is already in the sentence, waiting for you to learn it. To *imply* means to suggest that something is true without stating it clearly.

8. The squeaks made by bats are usually too high-pitched to be *perceived* by humans.
   a. imitated
   b. enjoyed
   c. noticed
   d. criticized

Did you choose *noticed*? Then you chose wisely. To *perceive* is to become aware of, recognize, or understand by means of the senses, such as hearing. You might have chosen *imitated* or *enjoyed*, both of which make sense, but don't accurately convey the entire meaning of *perceive*. They are more specialized, specific words, and here, the more general term *noticed* is the best choice.

9. Humor is the *predominant* theme of many animated television shows, including *The Simpsons*.
   a. most important
   b. interesting
   c. likeable
   d. controversial

You might have been able to decipher the meaning of *predominant* because it sounds similar to the word *dominate*, a word you might already know. The correct answer here is *a*. *Predominant* means "more noticeable, more prominent, having more power or more visibility than others." Context tells you that humor is one of several themes, so you might have chosen *b* or *c*, but the root word *dominant* confirms that the right choice is *a*. You'll learn more about root words in Lesson 6.

10. Almost every Saturday night Jeremy *implemented* a plan for sneaking out of the house late at night without his parents ever realizing that he was gone.
   a. planned
   b. succeeded
   c. put into action
   d. dreamed up

In this sentence, context tells you that Jeremy got out every Saturday night without being discovered. Thus, the correct answer is *c*. He did both plan and dream up the escape, and he did succeed, but only choice *c* describes *getting away with it*. To *implement* means *to make something happen*. In this case, your choice depended on your awareness of the word's connotation—you'll learn more about connotations in Lesson 4.

SUMMARY

This lesson gave you practice in figuring out word meaning from context. In the future, when you hear or read a word you don't know, instead of feeling frustrated or choosing to skip over the new word, use your meaning-from-context skills to figure out what the word means. You'll be pleased to find that often, you can teach yourself a new word just that easily!

Lesson 3 Words You Should Now Know

advocate	explicit
component	futile
context	implement
controversial	italicize
decipher	perceive
enigma	predominant

Extra Word(s) You Learned in This Lesson

_____

_____

_____

_____

create meaning from connotations

No one means all he says, and yet very few say all they mean,
for words are slippery and thought is viscous.
—HENRY BROOKS ADAMS (1838–1918)
AMERICAN NOVELIST AND HISTORIAN

This lesson will help you become more aware of how one word can convey several meanings. Becoming sensitive to the implied meaning of new vocabulary words will help you build your word power.

THE PREVIOUS LESSON focused on strategies for finding the meaning of words by looking closely at their context, or surroundings. In this lesson, you'll learn to identify subtle differences in the meanings of words that may seem quite similar at first.

At first glance, many words seem to convey the same thought, but upon closer inspection, you'll discover that this is not always the case. Words can *mean* very different things. We describe a word's meaning by using these two categories:

Denotation: the literal, dictionary definition of a word.

Connotation: the suggested, emotional, cultural, or implied meaning of a word.

Think about two simple words we all know and often use: *home* and *house*. Dictionary definitions of these words are quite similar:

> **house** (noun): a structure serving as an abode for human beings.
>
> **home** (noun): one's own dwelling place; the house or structure in which one lives; especially the house in which one lives with one's family; the habitual abode of one's family.

But, do the two words always mean the same thing? Look at the following sentences and consider the different uses of the word *home*.

> Israel is the ancestral home of many of the world's religions.
>
> Pedro is an American citizen, but he considers Mexico his home.
>
> The way home for the runaway is often long and lonely.

In each sentence, the word *home* means something different, something more subtle and complicated than the denotative meaning of a dwelling or a structure. In the second sentence, Pedro's emotional attachment to Mexico is great enough for him to think of it as home, a place of warmth, love, family, and happiness, even though he has an actual dwelling or abode somewhere in the United States.

In general, words have connotations that are positive or negative; sometimes a connotation is neutral, but this is less likely. Most often, words derive their connotations from the context in which they appear, or the way people use them. It's rare to use words only in their denotative, dictionary meaning, and because words can carry complicated meanings, it's important for you to be sensitive to their possible connotations. The more connotations you know, the stronger your word power will be.

PRACTICE 1: IDENTIFYING COMMON WORD CONNOTATIONS

Read the following sets of words, and then write each word in the appropriate column according to the connotation, or association, it has for you and your friends.

1. thin, plump, fat, slim

2. chatty, quiet, talkative, moody

3. snooty, friendly, vain, proud

4. shack, residence, apartment, condo

Positive Connotations	Negative Connotations	Neutral Connotations

How many words did you write in the *neutral* column? Did you hesitate about certain words? Is it fair to conclude that most words you use have a connotative meaning at least slightly different from their denotative meanings?

SAYING EXACTLY WHAT YOU MEAN

Whenever you speak or write, be aware of any connotations of the words you use. As you know, the words you choose convey your meaning; that's what language does. But not only words have connotations; whole sentences do. Spoken or written language that includes carefully chosen connotative words to convey emotions or subtle suggestions make sentences more interesting and help listeners or readers get a clearer understanding of what you're really trying to say. The more precise your words, the more power they will have, and the better your overall communication will be.

PRACTICE 2: CREATING MEANING THROUGH CONNOTATION

For each sentence below, identify the change in meaning created by the substitution or addition of a new word or words to describe the underlined word or words in the sentence. If you don't know a word, look it up in the dictionary. The example has been done to give you a sample to follow.

> **Example**
> The <u>candidate</u> raised his arms <u>above his head</u> as the crowd applauded <u>loudly</u>.
> The victorious candidate raised his arms heroically as the crowd applauded uproariously.
> **Denotation of the sentence:** A candidate won and the crowd applauded.
> **Connotation of new sentence:** An extremely popular candidate won and felt proud of his victory. This sentence is much richer in connotation; it communicates meaning more effectively.

Now, describe the differences between sentences by telling denotative and new connotative meanings. You may want to include a description of the writer's attitude toward the subject in each case.

1. <u>After</u> Hurricane Katrina, the city <u>ran out of</u> first aid supplies.

In the tragic wake of Hurricane Katrina, the city's first aid supplies were found to be inadequate and drastically lacking.

Denotation:_____

New Connotation:_____

2. The reviews of the movie *The Wizard of Oz* <u>varied</u>, but the audiences <u>liked</u> the movie.

The movie reviewers were ambiguous in their comments about *The Wizard of Oz*, but the audiences loved the movie unanimously.

Denotation:_____

New Connotation:_____

3. <u>Speaking</u> after a coughing fit is <u>hard</u>.

Speaking coherently after a coughing fit is often more than a cold sufferer can manage.

Denotation:_____

New Connotation:_____

4. Cutting school can <u>affect</u> your future.

The consequences of repeatedly cutting school can have negative repercussions throughout your life.

Denotation:_____

New Connotation:_____

5. The newspaper reporter was <u>accused of favoring</u> one candidate over the other.

The newspaper reporter was said to be guilty of distorting the facts in order to damage one candidate's reputation.

Denotation:_____

New Connotation:_____

Can you make a generalization about the difference between each of the first and second sentences? Do you see that the second sentences have more words, more specific words, and more complicated thoughts than the first sentences? As you've no doubt figured out, these are the characteristics of sentences with word power.

Lesson 4 Words You Should Now Know

ambiguous	distort
coherent	inadequate
connotation	subtle
consequence	unanimous
denotation	uproarious

Extra Word(s) You Learned in This Lesson

_____

_____

_____

_____

ANSWERS

Practice 2: Creating Meaning through Connotation

1. <u>After</u> Hurricane Katrina, the city <u>ran out of</u> first aid supplies.
   In the tragic wake of Hurricane Katrina, the city's first aid supplies were found to be inadequate and drastically lacking.
   Denotation: Factual report of lack of supplies.
   New Connotation: Sentence blames the city for running out of supplies by using emotional words like *tragic, inadequate,* and *drastically.*

2. The reviews of the movie *The Wizard of Oz* <u>varied</u>, but the audiences <u>liked</u> the movie.
   The movie reviewers were ambiguous in their comments about *The Wizard of Oz,* but the audiences loved the movie unanimously.
   Denotation: Interesting but unexplained report that reviews of movie varied.
   New Connotation: Sentence explains how popular movie was with audiences even though reviewers weren't clear about what they thought.

3. <u>Speaking</u> after a coughing fit is <u>hard</u>.
   Speaking coherently after a coughing fit is often more than a cold sufferer can manage.
   Denotation: Sentence states a fact, but that's all. No new information is provided.
   New Connotation: Sentence communicates what it is like to have a bad cold and cough.

4. Cutting school can <u>affect</u> your future.
   The consequences of cutting school repeatedly can have negative repercussions throughout your life.
   Denotation: Sentence makes an unclear statement what the effect of cutting school will be.
   New Connotation: Sentence is somewhat clearer by saying effect is negative for a long time.

5. The newspaper reporter was <u>accused of favoring</u> one candidate over the other.
   The newspaper reporter was said to be guilty of distorting the facts in order to damage one candidate's reputation.
   Denotation: Sentence is vague and doesn't explain how the reporter favored the candidate.
   New Connotation: Sentence more clearly says what the reporter did that was wrong and why he did it.

understanding word parts

Let language be the divining rod that finds the sources of thought.
—KARL KRAUS, (1874–1936)
AUSTRIAN WRITER AND JOURNALIST

This lesson helps build word power by providing practice in taking words apart. Knowing common prefixes and suffixes and how they work, you'll gain vocabulary fluency with unfamiliar words. And you'll learn to expand and modify words you already know!

YOU PROBABLY HAVEN'T thought much about how words are made up of parts, but did you know that you can often figure out the meaning of an unfamiliar word by looking at its component parts? Remember that word component? You learned it in Lesson 3. Well, the parts are usually fairly easy to identify. In general, words are made up of three parts:

- **Root.** The main part of a word, to which prefixes and suffixes are added.
- **Prefix.** The syllable(s) attached to the beginning of a word to alter or add to its meaning.
- **Suffix.** The syllable(s) attached to the end of a word to alter or add to its meaning.

In this lesson, we'll concentrate on prefixes and suffixes, and leave word roots for a later lesson. You've been using prefixes and suffixes all your life, probably without even noticing them, and you no doubt already know most of them.

PREFIXES

The word *prefix* itself uses a prefix (*pre-*), which means *before*. The prefix changes the meaning of the word root, which is *fix*. Here's how:

Fix: to place securely
Prefix: a syllable placed at the beginning of a word.

Knowing prefixes can help you figure out the meaning of an unfamiliar word (do you see the prefix on the word *unfamiliar*?) in the following ways:

- Prefixes help you know whether the word is positive or negative.
- Prefixes help you determine the meaning of a word through context.
- Prefixes help you figure out the meaning of a word by the meaning of the prefix.

Some Common Prefixes in Words You Probably Already Know

Here are some prefixes you probably use all the time, with examples of how they work.

anti, ant: opposite, against. Think of *antibiotics* and *antiwar*.
circ, circum: around, on all sides. Think of *circumference*.
co, com, con: with, together. Think of *cooperate* and *connect*.
dis: away from, reversal, not. Think of *dismiss* and *disrespect*.
mis: bad, wrong, opposite. Think of *misbehave* or *misspell*.
multi: many, multiple. Think of *multimedia* and *multiplication*.
pre: before. Think of *precaution*, *prevent*, and *predict*.
re: back, again. Think of *replace*, *recall*, and *rewind*.
super: above, over. Think of *superintendent* and *superior*.

SUFFIXES

Suffixes may not be as easy to use to figure out the meaning of words. Suffixes most often just change a word's part of speech. For example, the adjective *equal* becomes a noun, *equality*, when you add the suffix *-ity*. The verb *depend* becomes the adjective *dependable* when you add the suffix *-able*. The noun *beauty* becomes the verb *beautify* when you add the suffix *-ify*. Obviously, there are way too many suffixes, and they're too complicated for you to memorize them all. But don't be discouraged. Instead, just be aware of how they work, and look for them when you try to figure out a word's meaning.

Some Common Suffixes in Words You Probably Already Know

-able, -ible: capable or worthy of. Think of *remarkable* and *incredible*.

-an, -ian: one who is, characteristic of. Think of *politician*.

-ish: having the character of. Think of *childish* and *foolish*.

-ive: performing an action. Think of *cooperative* and *defensive*.

-ate: to make or become. Think of *irritate* or *frustrate*.

-ize: to cause to become. Think of *colonize* and *humanize*.

....

TIP: Don't be intimidated (scared or made to feel nervous) by prefixes and suffixes. Recognizing them can often help you figure out the meaning of an unfamiliar word and they build your word power when you use them to expand or modify words you already know.

....

PRACTICE: FIGURING OUT NEW WORDS FROM PREFIX AND SUFFIX CLUES

Circle the correct meaning for the italicized word in each sentence.

1. *Antecedent* means
   a. fighting against.
   b. looking after
   c. coming before.
   d. recent.

2. *Multifaceted* means
    a. two-faced.
    b. many-sided.
    c. cut into parts.
    d. chaotic.

3. *Consensus* means
    a. an individual's opinion.
    b. a counting of individuals.
    c. separate and dissimilar.
    d. general agreement by a group.

4. *Dubious* means
    a. one who doubts.
    b. to question.
    c. doubtful, questionable.
    d. to be uncertain.

5. *Agrarian* means
    a. incapable of making a decision.
    b. to cultivate.
    c. to be out of date.
    d. relating to the land or land ownership.

6. *Metamorphosis* means
    a. to transform.
    b. one who has changed.
    c. a transformation.
    d. capable of change.

7. To *reconcile* means to
    a. reestablish a relationship.
    b. move away from.
    c. out do
    d. prioritize.

8. *Subordinate* means
    a. under someone else's authority.
    b. organized according to rank.
    c. something ordinary or average.
    d. unrealistic, fantasy-like.

9. *Docile* means
    a. one who rears animals.
    b. one who manages domestic affairs.
    c. willing to obey, easily managed.
    d. to obey authority.

10. To *subjugate* means
    a. to be the subject of a sentence.
    b. to conquer, bring under control.
    c. to be surrounded on all sides.
    d. to drive away from the source.

Lesson 5 Words You Should Now Know

agrarian	metamorphosis
antecedent	multifaceted
consensus	reconcile
docile	subjugate
dubious	subordinate
intimidate	

Extra Word(s) You Learned in This Lesson

_____

_____

_____

_____

ANSWERS

Practice: Figuring Out New Words from Prefix and Suffix Clues

1. **c.** The prefix *ante-* means before. *Antecedent* means *that which precedes, or comes before.*
2. **b.** The prefix *multi-* means many. *Multifaceted* means *having many faces, being complex.*
3. **a.** The prefix *con-* means *with, together. Consensus* means *general agreement reached by a group.*
4. **c.** The suffix *-ous* means having the quality of. *Dubious* means *doubtful, questionable.*
5. **d.** The suffix *-ian* means one who is or does. *Agrarian* means *relating to or concerning land and its ownership.*
6. **c.** The suffix *-sis* means the process of. *Metamorphosis* means *a transformation, a change of form or function.*
7. **a.** The prefix *re-* means back, again. To *reconcile* means *to reestablish a close relationship, to bring back to harmony.*
8. **a.** The prefix *sub-* means under, beneath. As an adjective *subordinate* means *of a lower or inferior rank, or subject to the authority of others.* As a noun, it means *one that is subordinate to another.* As a verb, it means *to put in a lower or inferior rank, or to subdue.*
9. **d.** The suffix *-ile* means having the qualities of. *Docile* means *willing to obey, or easily managed.*
10. **b.** The prefix *sub-* means *under, beneath.* To *subjugate* means *to conquer, subdue, bring under control.*

take words down to their roots

A blow with a word strikes deeper than a blow with a sword.
—ROBERT BURTON (1577–1640)
ENGLISH AUTHOR AND CLERGYMAN

This lesson, like the previous one, will help you build word power by taking words apart. Roots are the building blocks of words, and knowing some common roots will help you to gain vocabulary fluency with unfamiliar words.

IN THE PREVIOUS lesson, you learned how prefixes and suffixes modify words. In this lesson, you'll focus on the root words to which prefixes and suffixes are attached. Our English language is a relatively new language in the history of the world, and it's one of the richest and most complicated. Its very newness is responsible for the great variety of English words in the language. Thousands of English words are built upon root words from other languages that have existed for thousands of years. English, as we speak it today, began about 400 or 500 years ago, so we're practically babies in the language game!

People who study the history and origin of words and languages are called *etymologists*. But you don't need to be an etymologist to benefit from knowing how words are formed and re-formed with word roots. As a student, your vocabulary skills will be enhanced (look up *enhanced* if you don't already know what it means) by learning some common root words. Once you do, you'll be able to use them to help you figure out the meaning of unfamiliar words.

The two most common sources for English words are Latin and Greek roots. You probably learned about these civilizations in school, so you know that Latin was the language spoken in ancient Rome more than 2,000 years ago. Latin spread throughout Europe and eventually developed, by about the seventeenth century, into modern languages spoken today, like English, French, Italian, Spanish, and Portuguese.

A SAMPLE LATIN ROOT AND ITS USE IN COMMON ENGLISH WORDS

Look at some of the many English words that have been built from one Latin root.

> *ced/ceed/cess*: Latin root for *to go, yield, stop*
>
> ante*ced*ent: that which comes before
>
> *cess*ation: a stopping, the end of something
>
> con*cede*: to admit something is true, to surrender
>
> ex*ceed*: to extend beyond
>
> pre*cede*: to come before
>
> pro*ceed*: to go forward
>
> pro*ced*ure: the act of proceeding, a process

You don't have to memorize Latin roots; that would be a huge task and could take years! But a list like the one above should help you see the relationships that exist between words and help you figure out meanings of similar-sounding words.

Ancient Greek is the other major original source of many English words. The language spoken in Greece today is descended (look up that word if you don't already know it) from earlier forms of Greek that date back to the thirteenth century B.C. Imagine how fascinating it is for etymologists to trace a modern word in English back through 3000 years of Greek usage!

A SAMPLE GREEK ROOT AND ITS USE IN COMMON ENGLISH WORDS

Look at some of the many English words that have been built from one Greek root.

chron: Greek root for *time*

ana*chron*ism: something that is out of date or placed in the wrong time

*chron*ic: continuing over a long time, or recurring

*chron*ology: the sequence of events in time

*chron*icle: a detailed record or description of past events

syn*chron*ize: to cause to occur at the same time

Now that you've seen samples of Latin and Greek roots and their descendants in modern English, take the following quiz to see how other roots are used in common words you may use every day.

PRACTICE: LEARNING NEW WORDS AND SEEING THEIR ROOTS

Circle the correct meaning for the italicized word in each sentence.

1. The Latin root *am* means *love*. An *amiable* person is
   a. talkative.
   b. truthful.
   c. well educated.
   d. friendly, good natured.

2. The Latin root *plac* means *to please*. A *complacent* person is one who
   a. makes frequent mistakes.
   b. is argumentative.
   c. is self-satisfied.
   d. is known to tell frequent lies.

3. The Latin root *luc/lum/lus* means *light*. A *lucid* argument is
   a. very clear and understandable.
   b. loosely held together.
   c. illogical.
   d. one that blames others.

4. The Latin root *qui* means *quiet*. A *quiescent* place is
  a. very isolated.
  b. very chaotic.
  c. very dangerous.
  d. very still and restful.

5. The Latin root *loc/loq/loqu* means *word, speech*. Something that is *eloquent* is
  a. dull and trite.
  b. expressed in an effective way.
  c. very old-fashioned.
  d. equally divided into parts.

6. The Greek word *auto* means *self*. To have *autonomy* means to
  a. have a lot of money.
  b. be independent.
  c. have courage.
  d. have strong opinions.

7. The Greek root *pas/pat/path* means *feeling, suffering, disease*. To have *empathy* is to
  a. give to others.
  b. have a love for others.
  c. identify with the feelings of others.
  d. be similar to others.

8. The Greek root *pseudo* means *false, fake*. The root *nom/nym* means *name*. A *pseudonym* is
  a. a false name.
  b. an ancient god or deity.
  c. a harsh sound.
  d. a long and boring speech.

9. The Greek root *dog/dox* means *opinion*. The suffix *-ic* means *having the quality of*. A person who is *dogmatic* is
  a. not in touch with reality.
  b. intolerant of other opinions.
  c. one who asserts opinions in an arrogant way.
  d. secretive and ungenerous.

10. The Greek root *phil* means *love* and the root *anthro/andro* means human. *Philanthropy* is

  a. the love of humankind.

  b. a preference for something in particular.

  c. using force to control others.

  d. spreading unkind rumors.

....

TIP: Even if you don't have a clue about what a new word means, look at it closely and see if it sounds similar to another word you know, or if it has parts similar to other words you know.

....

Lesson 6 Words You Should Now Know

amiable	enhance
anachronism	etymologist
autonomy	exceed
cessation	lucid
chronic	philanthropy
chronicle	precede
chronology	procedure
complacent	proceed
concede	pseudonym
dogma	quiescent
eloquent	synchronize
empathy	

Extra Word(s) You Learned in This Lesson

_____

_____

_____

_____

_____

_____

_____

_____

_____

_____

_____

_____

_____

_____

ANSWERS

Practice: Learning New Words and Seeing Their Roots

1. d. *Amiable* means friendly and agreeable, likeable.

2. c. *Complacent* means pleased or satisfied with oneself.

3. a. *Lucid* means very clear, easy to understand.

4. d. *Quiescent* means inactive, at rest.

5. b. *Eloquent* means expressed in a powerful or persuasive manner.

6. b. *Autonomy* means personal or political independence.

7. c. *Empathy* means understanding or identifying with another's feelings or situation.

8. a. A *pseudonym* is a fictitious name, as often used by a writer.

9. c. *Dogmatic* means asserting yourself in an absolute, arrogant way. *Dogma* means a doctrine or a set of principles or beliefs that one believes are absolutely true.

10. a. *Philanthropy* means love of humankind, or the voluntary actions to help others.

mnemonics: codes to help you spell words

Words are a wonderful form of communication, but they will never replace kisses and punches.
—ASHLEIGH BRILLIANT (1933–   )
AMERICAN AUTHOR AND CARTOONIST

This lesson gives you a break from learning new words. Instead, you'll find entertaining and helpful ways to remember words you already know, used to know, or wish you knew better!

HAVE YOU EVER had this experience: You learn a word, its definition, and how to spell it, but a day or a week later, you can't remember part or all of it? Sometimes the spelling stumps you, or the exact definition, or how the word fits into a common grouping. Don't worry—you're not alone. Many people forget them, so useful memory tricks have developed to be passed on from learner to learner.

These memory aids are called *mnemonics*, an English word from the Greek *mnemonikós*, which refers to the mind. To pronounce this word, ignore the beginning *m* and say it this way: *nih-MONN-icks*. There are several kinds of mnemonics, many of which use *rhyme*. Following is the mnemonic for remembering how many days there are in each month. You probably already know this one. Research shows that people find it so simple to memorize that they only need to read or hear it once, and it's permanently filed in their brains.

Thirty days has September,

April, June, and November;

All the rest have thirty-one

Excepting February alone,

Which has but twenty-eight,

'Till leap year gives it twenty-nine.

You probably also know this rhyming mnemonic about the discovery of the Americas:

In fourteen hundred ninety-two, Columbus sailed the ocean blue.

Another common type of mnemonic uses *acronyms* (AK-ruh-nihmz) to aid memory. An acronym uses the initial letters of a word or phrase as a key. Here are two different acronym mnemonics for remembering the names of the five Great Lakes:

HOMES: **H**uron, **O**ntario, **M**ichigan, **E**rie, **S**uperior

Sally **M**ade **H**enry **E**at **O**ranges: **S**uperior, **M**ichigan, **H**uron, **E**rie, **O**ntario

See how this works? Here are mnemonic acronyms for remembering the points of the compass:

Never **E**at **S**hredded **W**heat: **N**orth, **E**ast, **S**outh, **W**est

Do you want to remember the order for tuning the strings on a guitar? Try

Elephants **A**nd **D**onkeys **G**row **B**ig **E**ars: E, A, D, G, B, E

As you can see, mnemonics are often silly, but that may help you all the more. One of the most nonsensical and universally remembered mnemonics is a sentence that includes every letter of the alphabet, and is often used by people learning to type:

The quick brown fox jumps over the lazy dog.

MNEMONICS TO HELP YOU SPELL CORRECTLY

Here are some useful mnemonics to help you remember words with tricky or hard-to-remember spellings:

1. *stationery/stationary*
   stationery with an *e* is the word that uses writing paper, pens and **envelope**s
   stationary with an *a* is the word that describes something that is **park**ed, not moving

2. *principle/principal*
   The principal of your school is your **pal**
   A principle is a ru**le** to obey

3. *capital/capitol*
   The first letter of a sentence is always spelled with a **tall** letter.
   The capitol building has a **dome** on it.

4. *Necessary* is a tricky word to spell
   Never **E**at **C**hocolate; **E**at **S**alad, **S**andwiches, **A**nd **R**emain **Y**oung

5. *quiet/quite*
   Think of **E.T.**, who was a very *quiet* alien, but *quite* a sweet one.

6. *cemetery*
   Remember always that there are thr**ee e**'s in *cemetery*.

7. *accommodations*
   Hotel rooms always have two beds that look like two **M**s.

8. *desert/dessert*
   You always want more, so dessert has two **S**s.

9. *separate (not seperate)*
   To remember to spell *separate* correctly, memorize this mnemonic:
   Separate is **a rat** of a word to spell.

10. *Mnemonics* is a tricky word to spell.
    Mnemonics **N**eatly **E**liminate **M**y **N**emesis—**I**nsufficient **C**erebral **S**torage.
    nemesis means *an opponent or problem that cannot be overcome*
    cerebral means *of or relating to the brain*

PRACTICE: SPELLING TRICKY WORDS

Choose the correctly spelled words to fill in the blanks. Once you've checked your answers at the end of the lesson, create a mnemonic to help you remember each word's correct spelling. Write your mnemonics in the spaces provided.

1. The television commercial for Save Your Life Vitamins promotes the _____ that eating healthy food isn't enough to keep you healthy.
   a. bilief
   b. beleif
   c. belief
   d. bileef
   My mnemonic:_____

2. The doctor, who is the spokesman for Save Your Life Vitamins, has appeared on the cover of numerous _____.
   a. magazenes
   b. magazines
   c. magezenes
   d. magizines
   My mnemonic:_____

3. The Save Your Life Vitamin Corporation is now facing _____ for fraud.
   a. prosekution
   b. prossecution
   c. prosecution
   d. proseccution
   My mnemonic:_____

4. The chief executive in charge of the company is in a tough _____.
   a. situation
   b. sittuation
   c. situachun
   d. sitiation
   My mnemonic:_____

5. He sweated so much at the press conference that his skin looked

_____.
   a. clamby
   b. clamy
   c. clammy
   d. clammby
   My mnemonic:_____

6. The arresting officer in the case couldn't help being jealous of the executive's exorbitant _____.
   a. salerry
   b. salary
   c. sallary
   d. salery
   My mnemonic:_____

7. It was a _____ day for the police department when the arrest was finally made.
   a. supurb
   b. superb
   c. supirb
   d. sepurb
   My mnemonic:_____

8. Law _____ is not always an easy profession to enter.
   a. inforcement
   b. inforsment
   c. enforcement
   d. enforcemint
   My mnemonic:_____

9. The rewards of serving the community are thought to be a _____ substitute for high pay.
   a. terrific
   b. teriffic
   c. terific
   d. terriffic
   My mnemonic:_____

10. Her sister thinks about the characters on her favorite TV show so much
that it is becoming an _____.

  a. obsession

  b. obssession

  c. obsessian

  d. obsessiun

My mnemonic:_____

Lesson 7 Words You Should Now Know

acronym	mnemonic
capital	nemesis
capitol	principal
cerebral	principle

Extra Word(s) You Learned in This Lesson

_____

_____

_____

_____

_____

_____

_____

_____

ANSWERS

Practice: Spelling Tricky Words

1. **c.** belief
2. **b.** magazines
3. **c.** prosecution
4. **a.** situation
5. **c.** clammy
6. **b.** salary
7. **b.** superb
9. **c.** enforcement
9. **a.** terrific
10. **a.** obsession

synonyms and antonyms: similars and opposites

We have too many high sounding words,
and too few actions that correspond with them.
—ABIGAIL ADAMS (1744–1818)
WIFE OF JOHN ADAMS AND MOTHER OF JOHN QUINCY ADAMS,
TWO PRESIDENTS OF THE UNITED STATES

This lesson helps you build word power through a review of useful synonyms and antonyms, good for bulking up your vocabulary.

ALL WRITERS AND SPEAKERS eventually face a similar problem: What word(s) should I use to communicate exactly what I mean? How can I make myself clear? Will the person listening or reading understand my thoughts?

Choosing the right word is probably the most difficult part of both speaking and writing. Using just the right word is at the heart of everyone's wish to be understood. Therefore, the fundamental goal of this book is to help you choose wisely as you increase your word power. Knowing lots of words is the key: the more words you know, the better able you'll be to choose the right ones as you communicate.

Building a strong vocabulary isn't something you can do overnight. Learning new words and how to use them is a never-ending process. Someone who is a good listener and a careful reader will continue to learn new words throughout life, because there will always be new words to learn. Think of all the words you know related to computers and television. None of those words even existed a hundred years ago because computers and TVs didn't exist. So don't be discouraged about not knowing enough words; remember that the language is growing right along with you.

One of the genuine pleasures of building your vocabulary is learning all the different words that can communicate the same idea. How many times do you say, *You know what I mean?* or, *I mean. . . .* Each time you say that, you're introducing the idea that you're going to repeat your thought, using different words. We all do it because we all want to make ourselves understood, and we strive to find the right words to accomplish this. When we repeat a thought in different words, we usually use *synonyms*, one of the most useful devices in our language.

WHAT'S A SYNONYM?

You've already been introduced to the word *synonym* in Lesson 1. A common dictionary definition of the word is:

> a word having the same or nearly the same meaning as another in the language. Some synonyms for the word *happy* are *joyful*, *elated*, and *glad*.

Simple enough, right? You use synonyms all the time, even if you didn't always know the official name for them. You've also probably used the opposite of a synonym, an *antonym*, which is defined as:

> a word having a meaning opposite to that of another word. The word *wet* is an antonym of the word *dry*.

When you learn a new word, you may grasp its meaning by associating it with one of its synonyms that you already know. For example, what's another word for *decrease*? You know that *decrease* means *to make smaller*, and its antonym is *increase*. So what is one of its synonyms? A good synonym for *decrease* is *diminish*. Write a sentence here using the word *diminish*.

_____

Do you like the sentence you wrote any better because it uses *diminish* instead of *decrease*? Does it sound more important? More grown-up? More precise?

HOW TO FIND THE SYNONYM YOU NEED

Many writers turn to a thesaurus to find synonyms. As we warned before, however, using a thesaurus is tricky unless you already know the exact meaning of each synonym listed for a word. If you don't, you run the risk of picking a word with the wrong connotation, or even the wrong denotation. Review Lesson 4 if you're not confident about the difference between denotation and connotation.

If you feel the need for extra help when you write, use a dictionary. It can help you to see the subtle differences in how a word can be used. For even more help, check out a dictionary of synonyms and antonyms. These dictionaries define all the synonyms and antonyms so you're less likely to substitute a word that doesn't make sense.

PRACTICE 1: IDENTIFYING USEFUL SYNONYMS

Circle the answer that means the same as the underlined word in each sentence.

1. A funhouse mirror can really <u>distort</u> your image!
   a. deform
   b. disappear
   c. repeat
   d. extend

2. The price of gasoline <u>fluctuates</u> daily.
   a. spin out of control
   b. run faster
   c. change frequently
   d. disappear

3. Falling down when you're learning to ride a bicycle is <u>inevitable</u>.
   a. impossible
   b. certain to happen
   c. unequal
   d. uncertain

4. The teacher offered bonus points as an <u>incentive</u> to completing the homework.

   a. a goal

   b. a stimulus to action

   c. a deterrent

   d. a valuable

5. The iPod is an <u>innovation</u> in the recording of music.

   a. different from

   b. a new development

   c. a repetition

   d. a tested formula

PRACTICE 2: USING SYNONYMS IN SENTENCES

Now that you've learned five new words, write a sentence for each of them.

1. _____

2. _____

3. _____

4. _____

5. _____

PRACTICE 3: IDENTIFYING ANTONYMS

Circle the answer that means the opposite of the underlined word in each sentence.

1. The classroom was <u>chaotic</u> once the teacher left the room.

   a. confused

   b. messy

   c. entertaining

   d. orderly

2. The young man is so <u>naïve</u> that he believes everything he reads on the Internet.
   a. religious
   b. informed
   c. careful
   d. innocent

3. The kids <u>persisted</u> with their soccer game even though recess was over.
   a. continued in spite of resistance
   b. stopped
   c. insisted on
   d. resisted

4. The teacher <u>implied</u> that we'd have a pop quiz on Friday, but we won't know for certain until we get to class.
   a. explained exactly
   b. suggested
   c. asserted indirectly
   d. questioned

5. An orange is <u>analogous</u> to a clementine, another type of citrus fruit.
   a. different from
   b. similar
   c. the same as
   d. deceptive

PRACTICE 4: USING ANTONYMS IN SENTENCES

Now that you've learned five new words, write a sentence for each new word. Use the word itself or its antonym.

1. _____

2. _____

3. _____

4. _____

5. _____

Lesson 8 Words You Should Now Know:

analogous	incentive
chaotic	inevitable
diminish	innovation
fluctuate	naïve
imply	persist

Extra Word(s) You Learned in This Lesson:

_____

_____

_____

_____

_____

_____

_____

_____

ANSWERS

Practice 1: Identifying Useful Synonyms

1. a. To *distort* is to change the shape or sound of something.
2. c. To *fluctuate* is to change frequently.
3. b. Something that is *inevitable* is certain to happen.
4. b. An *incentive* is an encouragement or stimulus to action.
5. b. An *innovation* is an introduction of a new idea, a new process, a new method, or an invention.

Practice 3: Identifying Antonyms

1. **d.** *Chaotic* means in a state of confusion, without order.

2. **b.** *Naïve* means innocent, uneducated, and without artificiality.

3. **b.** To *persist* means to continue doing something even if it is difficult or not approved of by others.

4. **a.** To *imply* is to suggest something indirectly, without saying it precisely or exactly.

5. **a.** *Analogous* is an adjective that is used to describe something that is similar to another thing.

which is the right word?

*I never made a mistake in grammar but one in my life
and as soon as I done it I seen it.*
—CARL SANDBURG (1878–1967)
AMERICAN POET

This lesson focuses on some common yet confusing words you're likely to use
as you write and speak.

DO YOU KNOW the difference between *accept* and *except*? How about *duel*
and *dual*? Or the real show-stoppers, *affect* and *effect*? These are examples of
some of the most commonly misused words. Sometimes people get confused
because words such as these look similar, sound similar, and are often spelled
similarly. Other times, the mistakes occur because the meanings of the words
are just plain confusing. Whatever the cause of the confusion, you need to be
able to use these words correctly if you want a strong vocabulary.

Here are some categories of confusing words you need to use carefully
in order to use them correctly:

- **Homophone.** A word that's pronounced the same as another
  word but is different in spelling and meaning. Example: *carrot*
  and *karat* (the unit of measure for precious gems).
- **Homonym.** A word that is either spelled or sounds the same as
  another word, but has a different meaning. Example: *meet* and
  meat.

- **Commonly Confused Words.** There are many words that are frequently confused and used incorrectly. The confusion arises because the words use the same root, or sound similar, or have similar meanings.

SOME COMMON CONFUSING WORD PAIRS

The following list shows some of the most common homophones and confusing word pairs, along with brief definitions. Memorize these words and their meanings. Using them correctly is the sign of an educated, word-powerful person.

Confusing Word Groups	Brief Definitions
accept/except	to *accept* is to recognize or take on *except* means to exclude something
adapt/adopt	to *adapt* is to adjust or modify something to *adopt* is to take something or someone as one's own
affect/effect	to *affect* is to modify or change something *effect* is a noun that means the result
all ready/already	*all ready* is the state of being prepared *already* means by this time
all ways/always	*all ways* means every method or path *always* means forever, as in time
bibliography/biography	a *bibliography* is a list of books or other documents a *biography* is the story of one person's life
breath/breathe	*breath* is a noun describing the intake of air *breathe* is the verb, the process of using the air
dual/duel	*dual* means two, or double *duel* is a formal fight between opposing parties
ensure/insure	to *ensure* is to make something or some idea certain to *insure* is to make something certain in financial terms
disinterested/uninterested	to be *disinterested* is to have no opinion either way to be *uninterested* is to be not interested
persecute/prosecute	to *persecute* is to punish in an extreme manner to *prosecute* is to take legal action against someone
personal/personnel	*personal* means belonging to an individual *personnel* means all the employees in a company

Confusing Word Groups	Brief Definitions
precede/proceed	to *precede* is to go ahead of to *proceed* is to continue in the same direction
stationary/stationery	*stationary* means unmoving, still *stationery* is paper for correspondence
their/there/they're	*their* describes something belonging to them *there* is a description of a place where something is *they're* is a contraction of *they are*
weather/whether	*weather* refers to the conditions in the climate *whether* is a conjunction that means *or* or *perhaps*
who/whom	*who* is the substitute word for he, she, or they (subject) *whom* is the substitute for him, her, or them (object)
your/you're	*your* describes something that belongs to you *you're* is a contraction of *you are*

TIP: The only sure way to know the definitions and differences between confusing words is to memorize them. So pay close attention to the chart above and do the exercises carefully. They'll help you learn the words permanently, so you can use them easily and correctly.

PRACTICE 1: IDENTIFYING THE CORRECT IF CONFUSING WORD

Circle the correct word in each sentence. The answers at the end of the lesson include definitions for both word choices.

1. The students were convinced their teacher was (*persecuting/prosecuting*) them with way too much homework.

2. One of the assignments was to create a (*bibliography/biography*) of all the books the students had read during the school year.

3. The teacher's goal was to help the students (*adopt/adapt*) good study habits.

4. The students, on the other hand, had a (*duel/dual*) objective: they wanted less homework and longer summer vacations.

5. The teacher promised that the in-class essay she assigned would have no (*affect/effect*) on the students' final grades.

6. In an attempt to convince the teacher to change the assignment, the students argued that they had (*all ready/already*) done enough in-class writing for the week.

7. The teacher smiled and told the students to take a deep (*breath/breathe*) and begin their writing assignment.

8. The students decided to stop resisting the inevitable and start getting down to work on their (*personal/personnel*) essays.

9. (*Whether/Weather*) or not the students' essays were neatly written and legible, the teacher planned to read them carefully and comment on them.

10. The (*stationary/stationery*) desks where the students sat suddenly fell silent when the essay writing finally began.

PRACTICE 2: MATCHING CONFUSING WORDS WITH THEIR DEFINITIONS

Draw lines to match each confusing word with its definition.

Confusing Word	**Definition**
1. adapt	**a.** double
2. except	**b.** written clearly
3. persecute	**c.** have an effect on something
4. bibliography	**d.** punish
5. legible	**e.** exclude
6. dual	**f.** list of books
7. affect	**g.** modify or change
8. adopt	**h.** take legal action against
9. prosecute	**i.** go ahead or in front of
10. precede	**j.** take on as one's own

PRACTICE 3: USING CONFUSING WORDS IN SENTENCES

Fill in the blanks with words you've learned in this lesson.

1. Submitting school assignments in _____ form is always sure to get you halfway to your teacher's heart.

2. Authors often include a _____ at the end of their books in order to direct readers to additional resources on the same subject.

3. Jin and Lin, both from Beijing, were _____ by the Adams family last year.

4. To _____ to American ways, the girls have had to learn new customs as well as new words.

5. The _____ of studying regularly is often an improvement in your schoolwork.

6. _____schoolwork often suffers when athletes spend too much time on the field.

7. The teacher, _____ the students call Ms. Sunshine, always smiles and laughs at her students' jokes.

8. The mean girls in the classroom next door were _____ in trouble with their teacher.

9. The _____ of the Beatles usually starts with their beginnings in Liverpool.

10. Georgina, who claimed she only listened to classical music, was _____ in the Beatles.

Lesson 9 Words You Should Now Know

Confusing Word Pairs

accept/except	ensure/insure
adapt/adopt	disinterested/uninterested
affect/effect	persecute/prosecute
all ready/already	personal/personnel
all ways/always	their/there/they're
bibliography/biography	weather/whether
breath/breathe	who/whom
dual/duel	your/you're

Additional Vocabulary Words You Should Now Know

homonym   karat

homophone   legible

Extra Word(s) You Learned in This Lesson

_____

_____

_____

_____

ANSWERS

Practice 1: Identifying the Correct If Confusing Word

1. persecuting. To *persecute* is to punish unfairly; to *prosecute* is to take legal action against.

2. bibliography. A *bibliography* is a list of books; a *biography* is the story of one person's life.

3. adopt. To *adopt* is to take something or someone as one's own; to *adapt* is to adjust or modify something.

4. dual. *Dual* means two; a *duel* is a formal competition between two opponents.

5. effect. *Effect* is a noun meaning result; *affect* is a verb meaning to have an effect on someone or something.

6. already. *Already* describes a point in time; *all ready* means that everyone in a group is ready.

7. breath. *Breath* is a noun meaning the air inhaled or exhaled; *breathe* is a verb meaning the act of inhaling and exhaling.

8. personal. *Personal* means belonging to an individual; *personnel* means all the employees in a company.

9. Whether. *Whether* is a conjunction of uncertainty, if; *weather* is a noun meaning the conditions of the atmosphere of a given place at a given time.

10. stationary. *Stationary* means unmoving; *stationery* means writing paper.

Practice 2: Matching Confusing Words with Their Definitions

1. g
2. e
3. d
4. f
5. b
6. a
7. c
8. j
9. h
10. i

Practice 3: Using Confusing Words in Sentences

1. legible
2. bibliography
3. adopted
4. adapt
5. effect
6. their
7. whom
8. always
9. biography
10. uninterested

SECTION 2

use different parts of speech to increase word power

IT IS ALMOST IMPOSSIBLE to separate having a strong vocabulary from knowing the basics of good grammar. In this section you will learn how to use your knowledge of the four basic parts of speech to build an inventory of useful nouns, verbs, adjectives, and adverbs that will make your writing and speaking more powerful.

discover new nouns

*One forgets words as one forgets names. One's vocabulary
needs constant fertilizing or it will die.*
—EVELYN WAUGH (1903–1966)
ENGLISH AUTHOR AND NOVELIST

With this lesson, you'll begin to explore many paths to building your word power. You'll start with nouns, one of the four basic parts of speech, to acquire new words and methods for enriching your vocabulary.

AS YOU KNOW, every sentence must have at least a noun and a verb. The noun is the person, place, or thing doing the action in the sentence; the verb, of course, describes that action. There are common nouns, like *boy, girl, dog, city,* or *mountain.* And there are proper nouns that describe a specific person, place, or thing, like *Harry Potter, Chicago,* or *Mt. Rushmore.*

Nouns are easy enough, right? Well, they can get more complicated, and much more interesting, when your vocabulary expands to include *less common* nouns. Real word power lies in the ability to use lots of different words, but particularly the exactly right nouns, as subjects of your sentences.

As you're finding out through this book, there's no magic pill that can increase your vocabulary. You just have to read and listen a lot, and pay close attention to the words being used. Along the way, you'll acquire new words and, almost without realizing it, a new ease in writing and speaking.

TIP: Remember that it's often easy to figure out the meaning of a new word by its context.

DISCOVERING NEW NOUNS

1. Read the following paragraph and circle any words that are new to you. Pay special attention to their context in words around them, some of which appear in bold type.

> **Vacation Planning**
>
> Mabel was trying to organize her family's vacation, and somehow it was getting more complicated than she'd anticipated. The kids would be at Camp **Serenity** for the first two weeks after the **summer solstice**, and after that, she planned to take them to Seventeen Flags for a special treat. The **dilemma** was finding a **hotel** or a nearby **inn** that offered **accommodations** for two kids, a mom, a dad, two dogs, and three pet snakes. "Maybe you should consider a **boardinghouse** or a **bed-and-breakfast**," suggested her travel agent, "or try a **hostel**. Such an **establishment** might show you **clemency** or at least a little **mercy**."

Did you encounter any words you didn't know? If so, list them here:

_____ _____ _____

_____ _____ _____

_____ _____ _____

_____ _____ _____

The paragraph includes several nouns that are more or less synonymous. The text would not make much sense; however, if the writer had used the familiar word *hotel* repeatedly, even though most of the alternative words used are actually synonyms or near synonyms for it. In fact, the use of different nouns enabled the writer, in the words of the travel agent, to make several suggestions that potentially widened Mabel's search for a place where she and her family and pets could rest their weary bones.

PRACTICE 1: CREATING SENTENCES WITH NEW NOUNS

Of course you know the word *hotel*, but did you know all the others: *inn, bed-and-breakfast, boardinghouse,* and *establishment*? How about the words *serenity, solstice, clemency,* and *mercy*? Which of these words were unfamiliar to you?

Use your dictionary to learn meanings for the new words. Then write sentences using three of the words you've just learned.

1. _____

2. _____

3. _____

....

TIP: The few moments you take to look up a word in a dictionary can really pay off. You'll understand the meaning of the word and pump up your word power with just a tiny input of energy on your part!

....

Read the following paragraph and circle any words that are new to you. Pay special attention to the nouns in bold type.

Do You Want Fries With That?
The student council meeting turned into a near riot. The **argument** on the day's **agenda** was whether or not the school should allow fast food and soft drinks to be sold in the cafeteria. One **viewpoint** was that soft drinks and potato chips were fine but French fries weren't. Another **position** held that soft drinks were really bad, and presented a detailed **deposition** from a medical expert about the harm these drinks can cause. **Mediation** seemed necessary, but who should be the **arbiter** of food **policy**? The students or the school **district's administration**? Should a **referendum** to all concerned parties, including parents, be offered? Surely someone had to provide **amnesty** to the warring parties.

You've probably read or heard some of these words before. Others may have been understandable because of their context. And still others may be entirely new words. Do you see how the use of less common nouns adds zest and interest to the paragraph? How would it sound if simpler, more common nouns were substituted for the boldfaced words?

PRACTICE 2: WORD AND DEFINITION MATCHING

Draw lines to match each word on the left with its definition on the right.

1. mercy   **a.** intervention to bring settlement

2. deposition   **b.** decreasing of punishment; forgiveness

3. hostel   **c.** one who settles controversies

4. serenity   **d.** forgiveness, compassion

5. clemency   **e.** signed testimony by someone absent

6. advocate   **f.** vote by all parties concerned

7. mediation   **g.** inexpensive overnight lodging

8. referendum   **h.** person who speaks in support of an idea

9. arbiter   **i.** a plan of action of an organization

10. policy   **j.** state of calm, without disturbance

11. amnesty   **k.** choice between two unpleasant options

12. dilemma   **l.** safety from punishment or prosecution

PRACTICE 3: IDENTIFYING THE RIGHT NEW NOUNS

Directions: Fill in the blanks with words you've learned in this lesson, using the list in the preceding exercise as your inventory of possible nouns.

1. Some _____ was necessary in the committee room if the meeting was ever to end.

2. Congressman Jenkins, the committee chairman and the final _____, broke the tie vote and ended the heated argument.

3. The ideal political candidate has clearly presented _____ positions on most current issues.

4. The medical examiner, who was in the hospital and therefore could not attend the trial, sent in his written _____.

5. After one of the jurors started crying, the judge called for a recess in an attempt to institute a state of _____ in the courtroom.

6. The defendant, after being found guilty, begged the judge for _____ in determining the years he would have to spend in prison.

7. "Robbing a _____ is no less a crime than robbing a bank," declared the judge sternly.

8. The convicted robber's mother demanded _____ for her son, promising that he would change his ways in the future.

9. An _____ of lighter sentences for convicted robbers spoke to the courtroom in the young man's defense.

10. The judge reminded the audience that some prison terms were regulated by law, and that a _____, a vote of the citizens of the state, would be required to change the prison term rules.

Lesson 10 Words You Should Now Know

amnesty	mediation
arbiter	mercy
clemency	policy
deposition	referendum
dilemma	serenity
hostel	

Extra Word(s) You Learned in This Lesson

_____

_____

_____

_____

_____

_____

_____

_____

_____

_____

ANSWERS

Practice 2: Word and Definition Matching

1. d
2. e
3. g
4. j
5. b
6. h
7. a
8. f
9. c
10. i
11. l
12. k

Practice 3: Identifying the Right New Nouns

1. mediation
2. arbiter
3. policy
4. deposition
5. serenity
6. clemency
7. hostel
8. mercy
9. advocate
10. referendum

pick the best adjectives

The adjective is the banana peel of the parts of speech.
—CLIFTON FADIMAN (1904–1999)
AMERICAN EDITOR AND WRITER

This lesson brings you new and useful adjectives to strengthen your word power and make your communications more effective.

ADJECTIVES ARE WORDS that describe, modify, specify, or qualify a noun. Alas, the poor adjectives. They are so often undervalued, and thought of as little helpers to big, important nouns. But nothing could be further from the truth. *Adjectives just may be the most powerful, useful parts of speech in the whole language!*

Adjectives are the spice of language, the salsa on chips, the whipped cream on top, the special detail that tells listeners or readers what you really feel or mean. Here are some things adjectives do for communication:

- add color, definition, and detail
- clarify statements and explain new ideas
- paint visual images in the mind
- convey the emotions of the writer or speaker
- create emotions in the reader or listener
- help people win or lose arguments

Without adjectives, your language would be limp and lifeless, and it probably wouldn't give much useful information either. Consider the following sentences:

> Noah, my brother, brought home a dog.
>
> Noah, my youngest brother, brought home a dog.
>
> Noah, my youngest and silliest brother, brought home a darling little spotted puppy dog.

The first sentence provides facts, and that's it. You have no idea what kind of dog, or how the writer feels about the introduction of a dog to the home. The second sentence provides only a small additional piece of evidence—the writer's birth order in the family. The third sentence, however, gives you a lot of information. You learn the writer's opinion about his brother as well as his tendency to love dogs: the dog is no longer just a dog, but is now a darling little puppy.

Having an extensive vocabulary gives you the word power to apply the precise adjective(s) to convey the exact connotation you seek. Look at the following examples and note how the addition of more specific adjectives provides more interesting and exact meaning to simple phrases:

- a good movie
- a fun movie
- an action-packed adventure movie

- a hard vocabulary test
- a difficult vocabulary test
- a grueling vocabulary test

- a hard teacher
- a tough teacher
- a demanding teacher

In each group, the third sample provides the most information. The word *grueling* means *difficult or exhausting*. Use of the word is an obvious improvement over the acceptable, but not very interesting, adjective *difficult* to describe the test. Similarly, using the word *demanding* says a lot more about the teacher than simply calling him or her tough or hard.

SOME USEFUL ADJECTIVES FOR YOU TO LEARN

This lesson includes 12 very expressive and useful adjectives, along with short definitions and sample sentences to illustrate their meanings.

Read this list slowly and carefully to be sure you understand the words. If you can, think of a mnemonic to help you remember each meaning. Try to quickly come up with a sentence that includes that word.

1. *adjacent.* Next to. Our school is adjacent to a skate park where we spend afternoons.
2. *concurrent.* Happening at the same time. My two favorite television shows are concurrent, so I have to TiVo one or the other every week.
3. *eclectic.* Selected from a variety of sources. Our team consists of an eclectic mix of talented and totally untalented players.
4. *empirical.* Based on experience or observation rather than on ideas or beliefs. Weathermen use the empirical evidence found in historical records to predict future storms.
5. *finite.* Being limited; having an end or boundaries. Environmentalists believe Earth's resources are finite and must be preserved.
6. *implicit.* Suggested, implied, or understood; not directly stated. The teacher's implicit instructions were that neatness counted as much as timeliness, but she didn't say that exactly.
7. *inherent.* A natural part of something that cannot be separated from it. Competitiveness is probably inherent in athletes.
8. *intrinsic.* A basic part of the nature of something or someone. Bees are intrinsically attracted to sweet-smelling flowers, and humans seem to be intrinsically attracted to sweet-tasting foods.
9. *predominant.* The most common or important; most dominant. Saving energy has become a predominant issue in countries all over the world, not just in America.
10. *preliminary.* Happening before something that is more important. The preliminary trials for the Olympics are held throughout the world in order to select each country's finest athletes.
11. *prudent.* Using careful and sensible judgment. Prudent students start their homework early, and finish early, in order to leave time for other more entertaining activities.
12. *reluctant.* Hesitant or uncertain. Hikers should not be reluctant to admit their fears about steep paths and rocky ledges.

TIP: Sometimes you can remember a word better if you focus on its synonym, or even its antonym. Think about synonyms and antonyms whenever you're learning a new word.

PRACTICE: MATCHING ADJECTIVES WITH THEIR DEFINITIONS

Draw lines to match each adjective with its definition.

Adjective	Definition
1. implicit	**a.** based on observation
2. finite	**b.** the most common or important
3. adjacent	**c.** a natural, inseparable part of something
4. concurrent	**d.** having an end or boundaries
5. intrinsic	**e.** being basic to something
6. inherent	**f.** selected from a variety of sources
7. empirical	**g.** suggested but not stated directly
8. predominant	**h.** coming before something more important
9. reluctant	**i.** next to something
10. eclectic	**j.** exercising careful judgment
11. prudent	**k.** happening at the same time
12. preliminary	**l.** hesitant or uncertain

Lesson 11 Words You Should Now Know

adjacent	implicit
concurrent	inherent
demanding	intrinsic
eclectic	preliminary
empirical	prudent
finite	reluctant
grueling	

Extra Word(s) You Learned in This Lesson

_____

_____

_____

_____

_____

_____

_____

_____

_____

_____

_____

ANSWERS

Practice: Matching Adjectives with Their Definitions

1. g
2. d
3. i
4. k
5. e
6. c
7. a
8. b
9. l
10. f
11. j
12. h

zip up your verbs

After the verb "to Love," "to Help" is
the most beautiful verb in the world.
Bertha von Suttner (1843–1914)
Winner of Nobel Peace Prize in 1905

This lesson brings you new and versatile (useful in many ways) verbs to strengthen your word power so your communications become more effective.

WITHOUT VERBS, NOTHING would happen. Verbs are the engines of communication, describing the action taking place or the relationship between two people or things. And verbs also tell a reader or listener the time of the action: present, past, or future.

Verbs are such an essential part of communication that sometimes a verb can stand alone to communicate a whole idea:

Stop. Go. Smile. Hurry.

Even in one-word answers, the verb is understood although not spoken:

Have I made myself clear?
Yes. [Understood, not spoken: You have made yourself clear.]

When are you arriving?
Tomorrow. [Understood, not spoken: I will arrive tomorrow.]

WHAT DO VERBS DO?

The primary function of a verb is to describe a state of being (is, are, and so on) or an action taken by the subject (the main noun) in the sentence:

> Janet *is* my sister. (state of being)
> Janet *eats* some chocolate every single day. (action taken by subject)

As the powerhouse of every sentence, verbs are extremely important. With the right, strong, precise verb, your sentences can be very forceful and create a strong impression.

> Janet eats some chocolate every single day.
> Janet snacks on some chocolate every single day.
> Janet devours some chocolate every single day. (*devour* means to eat quickly, with great hunger)

The basic fact in these three sentences is the same, but the information and emotion communicated changes dramatically with the simple change of the verb. Do you think the word *devour* carries a positive or a negative connotation? Does the writer approve of Janet's chocolate obsession? You probably can't answer these questions without more context in additional sentences; the word *devour* could be an implied criticism or just an amusing way to describe Janet's chocolate habit.

What you can definitely be sure of is that having a broad vocabulary gives you the word power to choose strong, colorful, and precise verbs to convey the exact connotation you seek.

SOME VERSATILE VERBS FOR YOU TO LEARN

This lesson provides 12 very useful verbs to add to your vocabulary, along with short definitions and sample sentences that illustrate their meanings.

Read the list slowly and carefully to make sure you understand the words. If you can, think of a mnemonic to help you remember each word's meaning, or think quickly of a sentence using the word.

1. *allocate.* To set aside for a specific purpose. The teacher allocated 15 minutes each day to a review of new vocabulary words.

2. *attain*. To accomplish or achieve. Students who want to attain high marks must allocate time every evening to undisturbed study.

3. *augment*. To increase or add to. Readers seeking to augment their vocabulary will enjoy reading this book.

4. *cease*. To stop. The students' laughter ceased as soon as the tests were handed back.

5. *compensate*. To pay; to make up for something. 1. The teacher is compensated for her hard work with a yearly salary. 2. Many students tried to compensate for their lack of hard work by charming the teacher with smiles and jokes.

6. *compile*. To put together from various sources. The class compiled its new vocabulary list from several of the stories read in class.

7. *deduce*. To reach a conclusion using facts. The teacher was able to deduce which students had studied and which hadn't by the vocabulary test results.

8. *derive*. To receive or understand something from something or somewhere else. Many words in English are derived from roots that originated in Latin or Greek.

9. *interpret*. To explain; to translate from one form into another. The teacher interpreted the students' smiles to mean that they either enjoyed the lesson or were glad it was over!

10. *perceive*. To see or understand something that's difficult to understand. The serious students perceived the need to study hard; the others didn't.

11. *prioritize*. To organize or handle in order of importance. I prioritized my homework based on which assignments were due sooner than others.

12. *utilize*. To make use of. The teacher encouraged students to utilize their dictionaries to learn the accurate meanings of words.

SOME HELPFUL MNEMONICS

It's often easy to remember a word's meaning by creating a mnemonic for it. Here are a few that may help you with this lesson's verbs:

Allocate: to assign **ALL** to a new place
Deduce: to **DEDUCT** or subtract one idea from another

Compile: to make a **PILE** of things
Perceive: to **SEE** something is to per-**SEEVE** it
Utilize: to **USE** something **USEFUL**

Can you invent some others?

PRACTICE: KNOWING YOUR NEW VERBS

Circle the the correct meaning of the italicized word in each sentence.

1. To *compile* something is to
   a. appreciate it.
   b. value it.
   c. describe it.
   d. gather it.

2. To *derive* something is to
   a. expand it.
   b. understand it.
   c. clarify it.
   d. avoid it.

3. If you *allocate* something, you
   a. worry about it.
   b. understand it.
   c. assign it.
   d. forget it.

4. To *compensate* someone means to
   a. pay them.
   b. criticize them.
   c. flatter them.
   d. dismiss them.

5. To *deduce* something is to
   a. think negatively about it.
   b. wonder if it is true.
   c. fix it firmly.
   d. figure it out rationally.

6. When you *augment* your work, you are
   a. increasing it.
   b. finishing it.
   c. avoiding it.
   d. enjoying it.

7. To *perceive* something means to
   a. oppose it.
   b. damage it.
   c. understand it.
   d. forget it.

8. To *prioritize* a task means to
   a. not complete it.
   b. continue doing it.
   c. despise doing it.
   d. plan to do it first.

9. To *cease* doing something is to
   a. continue doing it.
   b. despise doing it.
   c. stop doing it.
   d. appreciate doing it.

10. To *attain* something is to
   a. achieve it.
   b. reject it.
   c. imitate it.
   d. expand it.

11. When you *interpret* something you
   a. ask for it.
   b. admire it.
   c. explain it.
   d. inquire about it.

12. To *utilize* something is to
   a. understand it.
   b. use it.
   c. imitate it.
   d. achieve it.

Lesson 12 Words You Should Now Know

allocate	deduce
attain	devour
augment	interpret
cease	prioritize
compensate	utilize
compile	versatile

Extra Words You Learned in This Lesson

_____

_____

_____

_____

_____

_____

_____

_____

_____

_____

_____

_____

ANSWERS

Practice: Knowing Your New Verbs

1. d
2. b
3. c
4. a
5. d
6. a
7. c
8. d
9. c
10. a
11. c
12. b

dress up verbs with adverbs

When ideas fail, words come in very handy.
JOHANN WOLFGANG VON GOETHE (1749–1832)
GERMAN PHILOSOPHER AND WRITER

This lesson reviews how easily you can make your writing and speech livelier and more interesting by adding adverbs, those handy words that help verbs communicate better.

AS YOU LEARNED in the previous lesson, verbs are the engines of communication; they describe the action in sentences. Adverbs are words that modify, or add more information about, a verb, an adjective, or another adverb. Here are some examples:

    shouting angrily
    carefully shredding papers
    smiling graciously
    write easily
    gratefully count your blessings
    run quickly

As the examples show, adverbs add flavor and punch to verbs. In fact, adverbs can be thought of as fuel to makes verb engines work better. Using adverbs to dress up and clarify your communications is a great way to increase your word power.

TIP: Learning how adverbs work may seem like just another grammar lesson, but don't be turned off. Knowing adverbs and how they work will help you build word power, which is why you're using this book, right?

ADVERBS AT WORK

Adverbs provide information about how, when, where, and to what extent something is happening in a sentence. Some adverbs function as intensifiers, modifying adjectives or other adverbs to add intensity, or strength, to the words. Here are some examples:

We almost won the game.
He nearly ate the whole thing.
She always arrives promptly.

Many adverbs are formed by adding the suffix *-ly* to adjectives. So the adjective quick becomes *quickly* and *lazy* becomes *lazily*. Making adverbs this way is an easy way to expand your word power; just think of an adjective, then change it to an adverb to make a verb more specific.

SOME COMMON ADVERB MISTAKES

There are some adjectives and adverbs that get confused and are often used incorrectly. Memorize their correct use. If you learn them well, and never make an error with them, you'll immediately be perceived as a writer or speaker with both good grammar *and* word power.

Here are the correct usages:

real = always an adjective
really = always an adverb

Studying regularly can make a real difference.
Reading really opens students' minds.

bad = always an adjective
badly = always an adverb

Lynne has a bad cold.
Jimmy did badly on his vocabulary test.

good = always an adjective
well = almost always an adverb, except when it describes health

Jimmy is usually a good student.
He didn't feel well on the day of the test.
The team played well in yesterday's game.

ADVERBS TO KNOW AND USE WELL

This lesson provides 12 very useful adverbs, many of which you may already know and use in their adjective form. They're accompanied by short definitions, in case you don't know the words already, and sample sentences.

Read the list carefully and think of ways you can incorporate (add) the words into your daily vocabulary. Too often we use the same old words over and over, without attempting to make our sentences more lively and decorated.

1. *energetically.* To do something with notable energy, dedication, or extra effort. *The students attacked the new science project energetically.*
2. *enthusiastically.* To do something with eagerness or intense feeling. *The class approached the lesson in cookie baking enthusiastically.*
3. *experimentally.* To follow established procedures in order to establish the truth or accuracy of something. *Lasers are being used experimentally to monitor sales in the school store.*
4. *expertly.* To do something with an extraordinary amount of skill and knowledge. *Spelling bees demand that students spell expertly and stay calm as well.*
5. *extremely.* To do something at a level beyond the norm. *The teacher was extremely patient with the noisy class.*
6. *frantically.* To do something in a rush or panic. *The fire alarm sent the students running frantically from the building.*
7. *sadly.* To do something out of unhappiness, distress, or regret. *Once the all-safe bell sounded, the students returned sadly to class; they had hoped for a day off from school.*

8. *successfully.* To do something that achieves a goal; to reach success. *The teacher successfully convinced the students that they needed vocabulary help.*

9. *suddenly.* To do something in a quick, unexpected way. *The cookies seemed to be taking a long time to bake, but suddenly they were golden brown and ready to devour.*

10. *swiftly.* To do something quickly. *The time passed swiftly during the movie; the students hardly realized how much time had passed.*

11. *thoughtfully.* To do something with care, deliberation, and dedicated thought. *The teacher thoughtfully excused the students early on Friday, figuring they needed a break after a long hard week.*

12. *vigorously.* To do something with energy and strength. *Despite being ten points behind, the team played vigorously until the end of the game.*

PRACTICE 1: USING ADVERBS CORRECTLY

Fill in the blanks with adverbs you've learned in this lesson. You may repeat adverbs in more than one sentence if you like, but be sure to consider all the adverbs.

1. The marathon runners dashed _____ toward the finish line.

2. The proud parents watched _____ to see if their girl would finish the race successfully.

3. The cheerleaders yelled _____ as the game neared its dramatic end.

4. The winning team cheered _____ as they squirted water over their coach's head.

5. The losing team marched _____ off the field at game's end.

6. The athletes trained _____ for months in advance of the Olympics.

7. Losing _____ is the sign of poor sportsmanship.

8. Being a generous winner is the sign of a _____ well-trained athlete.

9. Our team learned how to be _____ losers when they lost their final game.

10. Determined to win next season, the coach _____ promised the students a longer training period next year.

PRACTICE 2: USING TRICKY ADJECTIVES AND ADVERBS TO PERK UP YOUR WRITING

Directions: Write six sentences using the tricky adjectives and adverbs you learned in this lesson. You may use more than one adverb or adjective in each sentence if you like. Each sentence must include at least one of these words:

bad, badly, good, well, real, really

1. _____

2. _____

3. _____

4. _____

5. _____

6. _____

Lesson 13 Words You Should Now Know

bad/badly	incorporate
energetically	real/really
enthusiastically	sadly
experimentally	successfully
expertly	suddenly
extremely	swiftly
frantically	thoughtfully
good/well	vigorously

Extra Word(s) You Learned in This Lesson

_____

_____

_____

_____

_____

_____

_____

_____

_____

_____

_____

ANSWERS

Practice 1: Using Adverbs Correctly

1. swiftly
2. thoughtfully
3. frantically
4. enthusiastically
5. sadly
6. vigorously
7. badly
8. really
9. good
10. enthusiastically *or* thoughtfully

S E C T I O N 3

build word power in all subject areas

THIS SECTION OF 12 LESSONS forms the heart of the book. Here you will learn interesting, useful, and impressive new words in various subject areas. Think of an area of your life that interests you and you'll find ways here to increase your word power on those subjects.

words to describe personalities

> *Watch your thoughts; they become words. Watch your*
> *words; they become actions. Watch your actions; they*
> *become habits. Watch your habits; they become character.*
> *Watch your character; it becomes your destiny.*
>
> ANONYMOUS

Beginning with this lesson, you'll learn new words that are connected to different subjects. Let's start with words associated with various personality traits.

WE ALL LIKE to think of ourselves as unique individuals. And we are. There's no one exactly like you; you're truly one of a kind. But how do you describe other people? Your best friend? Your favorite cousin? Your teacher?

After you describe a person's physical characteristics (tall, short, blonde, and so on) it's likely you'll begin describing the person's personality traits. (A *trait* is a distinguishing characteristic or habit.) By naming one or more personality traits, you put the person into a category you're fairly confident your reader or listener will recognize. *My brother is a real jock; he lives for sports. My best friend is a fashion guru; she always has the latest styles. My mom is a compulsive cleaner; our house is so organized!* See how it works? Our minds automatically search for a category, or general description, that will best communicate our ideas about the person we're talking about.

This lesson gives you words to describe various personal characteristics or personality types. As you read, write down other words you think of that are associated with personality. Notice that some words are nouns and some are adjectives. Which words do you think your friends might use to describe you?

WORDS THAT DESCRIBE PERSONALITY TYPES AND TRAITS

1. *artistic.* Describes a person who has creative skills or serious interest in the arts. *Charles knew from an early age that his artistic interests would lead to a career as a painter.*

2. *altruist.* A person who is more interested in the welfare of others than in himself or herself. *Even young altruists are able to find programs to benefit from their charitable work.*

3. *egotist.* A person who is self-centered and thinks himself or herself better than others. *Cinderella's stepsisters were definitely egotists; they never considered the poor girl at all.*

4. *extrovert.* An outgoing, gregarious person who enjoys the company of others. *Mary Lou, secretary of the glee club and class president, is a fine example of an extrovert.*

5. *gourmet.* A person who is very serious about the quality of food—sometimes called a *foodie. My mother is an out-and-out gourmet; she loves to spend hours in the kitchen, and everything she makes is delicious.*

6. *introvert.* A person who is shy. *My parents think I'm an introvert because I like spending a lot of time reading by myself.*

7. *laconic.* A person who uses as few words as possible to communicate ideas. *My teenage brother has become dramatically laconic; he rarely speaks, and usually only grunts.*

8. *loner.* A person who prefers to be alone, and avoids the company of others. *We've never met our next door neighbor; we refer to him as The Loner of Lambert Lane.*

9. *loquacious.* Describes a person who is very chatty and talkative. *My friend Jennie is always in trouble at school because she's so loquacious.*

10. *narcissist.* A person who thinks only of himself or herself. *The country's dictator was a terrible narcissist; he didn't care at all for the welfare of his people.*

11. *pretentious.* Describes a person who is always trying to impress others and pretends to be very important or wise. *It is very pretentious to use big words when small ones will communicate just as well.*

12. *prodigy.* A person, usually quite young, who is unusually talented or gifted. *Jonathan, a true chess prodigy, won his first national competition at age five.*

PRACTICE 1: IDENTIFYING PERSONALITY TYPES

Fill in each blank with the word from this lesson that fits the personality type being described. The first letter of each correct answer has been provided.

1. Jim is always chatting.   l_____

2. Sandy prefers his own company.   i_____

3. Lynne enjoys cooking as much as eating.   g_____

4. Jon speaks in very short sentences.   l_____

5. Sandy's twin also sticks to himself.   l_____

6. Suzanne likes to show off her vocabulary.   p_____

7. Peter says he lives to help others.   a_____

8. Dianne dreams of becoming a sculptor.   a_____

9. Jim is always admiring himself in the mirror.   n_____

10. Marianne loves being with people.   e_____

11. Alfie thinks he is better than others.   e_____

12. Young Sam won every race he entered.   p_____

PRACTICE 2: RETESTING YOUR VOCABULARY KNOWLEDGE

Do the following sentences use this lesson's words correctly? Write T (for *true*) if a boldfaced word is used correctly and F (for *false*) if it is not. Read carefully; there may be tricks in the statements.

_____ 1. **Loners** are people who never seem to prefer their own company.

_____ 2. People who tend to speak in short sentences or who prefer not to speak much at all are described as **narcissists**.

_____ 3. Girls are often described as being **loquacious** because they chat a lot.

_____ 4. If you use a lot of fancy words, you may be accused of being an **egotist**.

_____ 5. If you spend more time in museums than you do at the movies, you can definitely be characterized as an **artistic** person.

_____ 6. Using longer words instead of shorter ones is a common habit among **pretentious** people.

_____ 7. The young pianist so hated being with other people that even newspaper articles about him described him as an **introvert**.

_____ 8. The **gourmet** chef made his reputation working at a small town diner.

_____ 9. Being an **extrovert** means that you are probably most concerned with yourself and don't have much time to extend outward.

_____ 10. When your idea of a vacation is to go to New Orleans and help rebuild houses, you are probably known as an **altruist**.

_____ 11. **Egotists** are people who are said to think of themselves before they think of others.

_____ 12. By the age of ten, the mathematics **prodigy** was scoring better on college-level calculus exams than the university students.

PRACTICE 3: WHO ARE YOU?

Fill in the first sentence about yourself using one or more of the words from this lesson. Use the second sentence to describe a sister or brother, best friend, teacher, or parent.

You may use additional words not found in this lesson.

1. I would describe myself as a _____ because I _____

_____

_____

2. I would describe _____ as a _____ because
he/she_____

_____

_____

Lesson 14 Words You Should Now Know

altruistic	extrovert
laconic	narcissist
artistic	gourmet
loner	pretentious
egotist	introvert
loquacious	prodigy

Extra Word(s) You Learned in This Lesson

_____

_____

_____

_____

ANSWERS

Practice 1: Identifying Personality Types

1. loquacious
2. introvert
3. gourmet
4. laconic
5. loner
6. pretentious
7. altruist
8. artistic
9. narcissist
10. extrovert
11. egotist
12. prodigy

Practice 2: Retesting Your Vocabulary Knowledge

1. F
2. F
3. T
4. F
5. T
6. T
7. T
8. F
9. F
10. T
11. T
12. T

words to describe feelings

Human vocabulary is still not capable, and probably never will be, of knowing, recognizing, and communicating everything that can be humanly experienced and felt.

José de Sousa Saramago (1922–   )
Portuguese novelist and Nobel Prize winner

In this lesson, you'll learn new words to describe feelings and emotions. This will help you build a vocabulary inventory of words for these hard-to-describe experiences.

PROBABLY THE MOST common word search for speakers and writers is the hunt for the perfect word to express an emotion they're feeling. It happens to all of us at one time or another. We want to explain what or why we feel or think the way we do, but can't seem to find the right words to express our ideas.

Reread the quotation at the opening of this lesson by José Saramago. He's known for his use of very simple words, but as a writer, he also experiences the difficulty of finding the precise word to describe a particular emotion. There are thousands of words to choose from, and they can help us try to convey what we're thinking and feeling. That's what communication is, after all: the exchange, however imperfect, of facts, ideas, and emotions.

In this lesson, you'll learn some common and useful words for describing various emotions. As you read the list, write down any other words that pop into your head—words you use, or are not sure how to use, to describe feelings you've had.

TIP: Take time to look up new words in a dictionary. Once you've looked up a word, try to use it right away to make it a permanent part of your personal word bank.

WORDS THAT DESCRIBE EMOTIONS AND FEELINGS

1. *apathetic.* Lazy, uninterested, indifferent. *The long, hot summer and the lack of friends nearby made the sisters bored and apathetic.*
2. *dejected.* Sad, disappointed, pessimistic. *The candidate was visibly dejected when it became clear he had lost the election.*
3. *ecstatic.* Extraordinarily joyous. *The winning candidate's ecstatic victory speech was greeted by cheers from the crowd of supporters.*
4. *elated.* Delighted, pleased. Slightly less joyful than ecstatic, but showing great happiness. *The kids were elated when their parents announced a spring trip to Disneyland.*
5. *frustrated.* Disappointed or unhappy because of an inability to achieve a goal or fulfill a desire. *John was frustrated by his inability to score higher on his math test, no matter how much time he spent studying for it.*
6. *humiliated.* Strongly embarrassed. *The figure skater was humiliated when, after landing a triple loop jump, she then tripped over her own skate laces.*
7. *lonely.* Unhappy because of lack of access to other people; feeling empty. *Spending the summer in the mountains was fun for the parents, but lonely for the kids, who missed their friends and sports activities.*
8. *melancholy.* Extremely sad or depressed, for some period of time. *Jane's melancholy was interrupted, finally, by the visit of her best friend and their plans for a trip together.*
9. *patriotic.* Loving of one's country, a feeling often associated with unselfish sacrifice. *The soldiers served their country with patriotic enthusiasm, despite the risks to their lives.*
10. *prudent.* Cautious and practical in making decisions. *The prudent climbers listened to the advice of their guide as they made their ascent up Mt. Everest.*

11. *timid.* Exhibiting a lack of confidence, an extreme shyness. *I was a bit timid about trying to ride a skateboard, but discovered that when I used caution, it was fun!*

12. *vindictive.* Feeling a strong desire for revenge and to do harm to another. *The class bully was vindictive and disruptive, which alarmed the other students and frustrated the teacher.*

PRACTICE 1: IDENTIFYING WORDS THAT DESCRIBE EMOTIONS

Fill in each blank with the word from this lesson that fits the emotion or feeling being described. The first letter of each correct answer is provided.

1. Tom spends lot of time by himself, which makes him sad.   l_____

2. Sharon is shy and afraid to speak.   t_____

3. Jim is always careful about choices.   p_____

4. Ms. Price is thrilled with her new job.   e_____

5. Ethan's mood is always sad, no matter what.   m_____

6. Colin's first loyalty is to his country.   p_____

7. Carol is known to be mean to her enemies.   v_____

8. Sam remains sad over his bad school grades.   d_____

9. Jerry was delighted to win $1,000,000.   e_____

10. John is disappointed that he can't enter the race. f_____

PRACTICE 2: EMOTIONS AND FEELINGS CROSSWORD PUZZLE

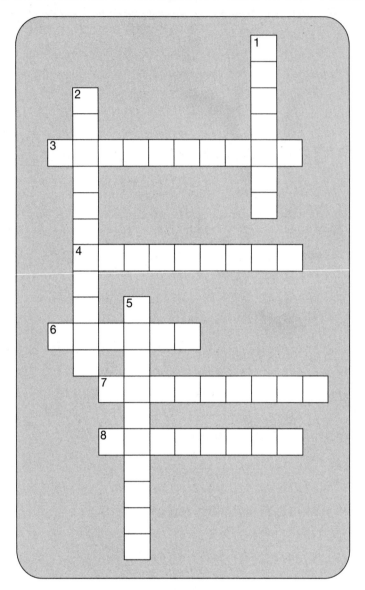

Across

3 embarrassed in front of others
4 uninterested in any activity
6 preference for one's own company
7 love of country
8 extraordinary joy

Down

1 careful; cautious about choices and decisions
2 unhappiness at not achieving a goal
5 continuing sadness and depression

Word Bank

apathetic	lonely
ecstatic	melancholy
frustration	patriotic
humiliated	prudent

Lesson 15 Words You Should Now Know

apathetic	lonely
dejected	melancholy
ecstatic	patriotic
elated	timid
frustrated	vindictive
humiliated	

Extra Words You Have Learned in This Lesson

_____

_____

_____

_____

ANSWERS

Practice 1: Identifying Words That Describe Emotions

1. lonely
2. timid
3. prudent
4. elated
5. melancholy
6. patriotic
7. vindictive
8. dejected
9. ecstatic
10. frustrated

Practice 2: Emotions and Feelings Crossword Puzzle

Across
3 humiliated
4 apathetic
6 lonely
7 patriotic
8 ecstatic

Down
1 prudent
2 frustration
5 melancholy

L E S S O N 16

words to describe extreme emotions

It is with words as with sunbeams—the more they are condensed, the deeper they burn.
ROBERT SOUTHEY (1774–1843)
ENGLISH POET LAUREATE

In this lesson, you'll discover more words to describe feelings and emotions, especially those that describe intense or extreme experiences.

ARE YOU FRUSTRATED when you try to describe how much you hate homework or the noise from the people next door? Or when you try to tell your parents how much you love them?

Do you ever sputter and stammer when you want to explain exactly why you dislike spiders, no matter how small they are?

Is it hard for you to explain exactly why you like your favorite singer or your favorite team or your favorite book?

You're not alone. Our strongest emotions are the most complicated. As you learned in the previous lesson, there are thousands of words you could use to explain what you're thinking and feeling, both for yourself and when you want to describe your emotions and beliefs to others. *The better able you are to define your emotions, the stronger your word power will be, and the better able you'll be to communicate with others.*

TIP: Remember that many words have different grammatical forms, so learning one word may really mean you've learned several. Think of the word *anger*. As a noun, it describes a strong feeling of displeasure. As a verb, it describes the act of making someone else angry. And in its adjective form, *angry*, it describes the person feeling the extreme displeasure.

Here are some useful words to describe extreme feelings. As you read the list, write down any additional words you can think of to describe strong emotions you've had.

WORDS THAT DESCRIBE EXTREME EMOTIONS

1. *contempt.* The feeling that someone or something is inferior or not worthy of respect; the state of being thought of as inferior. *Some major league players feel contempt for minor league players who have ambitions for greater glory.*
2. *delirious.* The feeling of uncontrolled excitement or happiness. *The cheerleaders were delirious with joy when their team made it to the finals.*
3. *despise.* To think of something or someone with contempt, hatred, or disgust. *The coach despised his team's lack of commitment to regular practice.*
4. *envy.* To be unhappy because someone else has possessions or qualities. *The elementary school students envied the middle school kids' privileges at recess and lunchtime.*
5. *furious.* Filled with rage or fury; full of energy or speed, as in a furious storm. *The teacher was furious when all the students failed to do their homework, and the students were equally furious when the teacher assigned them another essay to write.*
6. *gluttonous.* Eating excessively, or doing things to an extreme. *The team mascot, who loved to make jokes on himself, was considered a glutton for punishment.*
7. *horrified.* Intensely fearful or revolted by something or someone. *The parents were horrified by their children's love of horror movies.*

8. *jealous*. Feeling resentment because of another person's success, qualities, or possessions. *The pep squad seemed jealous of all the attention the cheerleaders got when they appeared in new uniforms.*

9. *obsessed*. Having intense or excessive interest or concern for something or someone. *The team was obsessed with the idea of making the final playoffs.*

10. *petrified*. Being so frightened that one is unable to move. *The thought of losing three games in a row petrified the team, and so they arranged an extra practice session.*

11. *prejudiced*. Having a strong opinion without consideration of the facts; creating a negative impact on someone else. *The community was prejudiced about raising taxes, fearing that homeowners with lower incomes would feel they were being prejudiced.*

12. *terrified*. Being seriously frightened; seriously frightening someone else. *The popularity of horror movies suggests that many movie fans love being terrified.*

PRACTICE 1: TESTING YOUR VOCABULARY KNOWLEDGE

Do the following sentences use this lesson's boldfaced vocabulary words correctly? Write T if a boldfaced word is used correctly and F if it is not. Read carefully; there may be tricks in the statements.

_____ 1. Being **horrified** is one of the true pleasures of being a fan of the *Alien* movies.

_____ 2. Feeling **envy** is a common emotion that describes feeling charitable and generous to others.

_____ 3. If you **despise** a group of people, you are being thoughtful and considerate.

_____ 4. If you have **contempt** for a group of people, you consider them inferior and less worthy than yourself.

_____ 5. Being **jealous** is feeling negative or hostile about the fact that someone else has something that you don't have.

_____ 6. A **glutton** is someone who envies others.

_____ **7.** Weddings are events usually filled with **delirious** emotions.

_____ **8.** Barking dogs are usually **furious** about being kept tied up.

_____ **9.** Being **prejudiced** about another group is not always a sign of igno-
rance.

_____ **10.** To be **petrified** of snakes is usually a safe plan when you're in the
desert.

_____ **11.** If you are **obsessed** with becoming rich, you may miss many of
life's cheap pleasures.

_____ **12.** Being **terrified** of tests is usually the sign of being unprepared to
do well on them.

PRACTICE 2: IDENTIFYING STRONG EMOTIONS

Fill in each blank with the word from this lesson that fits the description. The
first letter of each correct answer has been provided.

1. Jane wishes she had as many friends as Stacy.   e_____

2. Tom is very scared of losing a match.   t_____

3. Suzanne thinks her siblings are idiots.   c_____

4. Sid's desire to eat is out of control.   g_____

5. Jim hates that his brother is smarter than he.   j_____

6. The bride is crazy about her groom.   o_____

7. The team's victory made them joyous.   d_____

8. Cats are usually thought to hate dogs violently.   d_____

9. The coach was really angry about the team's work.   f_____

10. The huge snakes scared the children.   p_____

11. The monster's size shocked the town.   h_____

12. Sam was certain the other team was weak.   p_____

Lesson 16 Words You Should Now Know

contempt	horrified
delirious	jealous
despise	obsessed
envy	petrified
furious	prejudiced
gluttonous	terrified

Extra Words You Learned in this Lesson

_____

_____

_____

_____

ANSWERS

Practice 1: Testing Your Vocabulary Knowledge

1. T
2. F
3. F
4. T
5. T
6. F
7. T
8. T
9. F
10. T
11. T
12. T

Practice 2: Identifying Strong Emotions

1. envy
2. terrified
3. contempt
4. gluttonous
5. jealous
6. obsessed
7. delirious
8. despise
9. furious
10. petrified
11. horrified
12. prejudiced

strange feelings and emotions

How often misused words generate misleading thoughts.
HERBERT SPENCER (1820–1903)
ENGLISH PHILOSOPHER AND POLITICIAN

This lesson offers a list of words that describe rare emotions—feelings not common to all of us. Nevertheless, these are words that you will hear or read about and will enjoy adding to your vocabulary word power.

DO YOU EVER feel scared in an elevator or other small space?

Do you get dizzy when you look down from a tall building?

Do you sometimes suspect the whole world is against you?

Do you often think you may be sick, even when you have no particular pains?

Many people have these feelings once in a while. But when such intense feelings become a constant problem and affect people's everyday lives, these rare (not often found) fears are called *phobias.*

The dictionary definition of *phobia* is *an irrational fear of something that in normal circumstances poses little or no real danger.* If the problem continues, psychologists and other doctors have several ways to help people overcome their fears. But for the great majority of people, such fears aren't a problem; the people just feel strange when they occur.

These are special words that describe serious conditions, but these same words are often used in daily conversations to describe the occasional, infrequent fear people have. You can build your word power by learning interesting words to describe phobias or other strange behavior patterns. And because these words describe such odd emotions or behaviors, they're fun to know. Just be careful when you use them; they may be misinterpreted as an insult if you use them inappropriately.

TIP: Remember that learning one word often means learning two or more. For example, the inability to sleep is called *insomnia*; the person who suffers with this problem is called an *insomniac*.

WORDS THAT DESCRIBE STRANGE OR RARE EMOTION

1. *acrophobia.* Fear of heights. *The steep trail down the Grand Canyon terrified Judy, who had suffered from acrophobia her whole life.*
2. *amnesia.* The loss of memory. *The pilot recovered from the crash, but suffered amnesia about the details of his accident.*
3. *claustrophobia.* Fear of small spaces, like elevators or closets. *Air travel is an impossibility for my cousin Rebecca, who suffers from extreme claustrophobia.*
4. *arachnophobia.* An extreme fear of spiders. *My friend has arachnophobia to such an extent that she wasn't able to watch the movie* Charlotte's Web *at our sleepover last weekend.*
5. *hypochondria.* Excessive concern or talk about one's health, usually with concentration on a particular form of illness. *Everyone in the chess club is tired of Ethan's hypochondria; he always worries about the back pain he fears he'll develop at the chess contest finals.*
6. *insomnia.* Inability to sleep. *James decided that his insomnia was a blessing once he realized how much studying he could get done in the middle of the night when the house was quiet.*
7. *kleptomania.* A compulsion to steal, even without need or any specific desire. *The store manager accused his favorite employee of kleptomania after catching him shoplifting CDs three days in a row.*
8. *megalomania.* An obsession with grandiose or extravagant things or actions. *Many of the world's greatest generals are thought*

*to have been megalomaniacs who accomplished great victories pre-
cisely because of their drive to do grand things.*

9. *paranoia.* Extreme, irrational distrust of others. *Jason's paranoia
that the other students didn't like him was definitely unreasonable;
the other kids simply didn't know him.*

10. *pyromania.* An uncontrollable desire to set fires. *Park rangers con-
firm that forest fires are caused more often by careless mistakes than
by deliberate fires set by pyromaniacs.*

11. *agoraphobia.* An abnormal fear of open spaces, crowds, and public areas. This is the opposite of *claustrophobia.*

12. *vertigo.* A sensation of dizziness or spinning, even when standing or sitting on solid ground. *Vertigo is often associated with fear
of heights. Tom chose not to climb to the top of the Statue of Liberty
because he feared his vertigo might return.*

Lesson 17 Words You Should Now Know

acrophobia	kleptomania
agoraphobia	megalomania
amnesia	paranoia
arachnophobia	phobia
claustrophobia	pyromania
hypochondria	rare
insomnia	vertigo

Extra Words You Learned in This Lesson

_____

_____

_____

_____

_____

_____

_____

PRACTICE 1: MATCHING THE PROBLEM WITH ITS NAME

Draw lines to match the name of each problem with the area of its concern.

Name of Problem	Area of Concern
1. paranoia	a. fire
2. insomnia	b. small enclosed spaces
3. vertigo	c. illness
4. pyromania	d. sleep
5. claustrophobia	e. motives of others
6. hypochondria	f. dizziness
7. kleptomania	g. loss of memory
8. amnesia	h. high places
9. arachnophobia	i. stealing
10. acrophobia	j. spiders
11. agoraphobia	k. extravagant things
12. megalomania	l. open spaces

PRACTICE 2: STRANGE EMOTIONS CROSSWORD PUZZLE

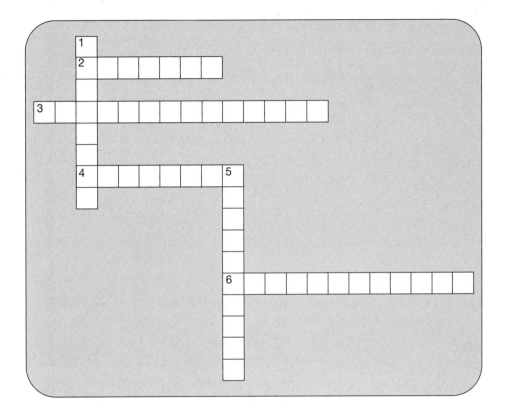

Across

2 total loss of memory
3 fear of small places
4 inability to sleep
6 excessive health concerns

Down

1 extreme distrust of the motives of others
5 fear of heights

Word Bank

acrophobia
amnesia
claustrophobia

hypochondria
insomnia
paranoia

ANSWERS

Practice 1: Matching the Problem with Its Name

1. e
2. d
3. f
4. a
5. b
6. c
7. i
8. g
9. j
10. h

Practice 2: Strange Emotions Crossword Puzzle

Across
2 amnesia
3 claustrophobia
4 insomnia
6 hypochondria

Down
1 paranoia
5 acrophobia

learn words for the sciences

We live in a time when the words "impossible" and "unsolvable"
are no longer part of the scientific community's vocabulary.
CHRISTOPHER REEVE (1952–2004)
AMERICAN ACTOR AND MEDICAL RESEARCH ACTIVIST

This lesson presents words from various fields of scientific study, and in so doing, reminds you of the value of identifying root words.

DO YOU LIKE taking things apart and putting them back together?

Do you like solving puzzles and other problems?

Do you like organizing things and putting them into categories?

If you answered yes to any of these questions, you may well be headed for a career in science. But which branch of science? There are literally dozens, if not hundreds. Indeed, our twenty-first century can be called a scientific century, one in which the contributions of scientific findings will change, and hopefully improve, our lives forever.

The different areas of scientific study are called *disciplines*, or fields of knowledge. Each addresses a specific area of knowledge. Once you begin to study one discipline, you'll find you can go deeper, and narrow your studies to an even smaller area of that science. For example, some entomologists— who study insects—specialize, spending their whole careers studying just caterpillars, or butterflies, or ants.

As you learn the words for the various areas of science, note that almost all of them share the suffix *-ology*. It comes from the Greek *logos,* which means *the study of.* Whenever you see a word ending in *-ology,* you'll know that the word describes a particular area of scientific study.

TIP: Note that professionals in each of these fields share the suffix *-ist,* added to a variation of the scientific-study word. Thus, a person working in the field of anthropology is called an *anthropologist.* You, as a person studying words, might be called an amateur *philologist*!

WORDS THAT DESCRIBE AREAS OF SCIENTIFIC STUDY

The words in this list by no means include all of the sciences. As you read the list, think of other areas of study that might interest you or that sound familiar. Jot them down, and then look up the definitions in your dictionary or use a search engine on the Internet.

1. *anthropology* (from the Greek *anthros,* meaning *humanity*). The study of the origins, customs, beliefs, and social relationships of groups of human beings. *The anthropologists studied the arrival thousands of years ago of early Native Americans to the North American continent.*

2. *astronomy* (from the Greek *astron,* meaning *star* plus the Greek *nomos,* meaning *arranging*). The study of outer space, especially the examination of all material objects and phenomena outside the earth's atmosphere. *The American commitment to exploration of outer space is an extension of the science of astronomy.*

3. *biology* (from the Greek *bios,* meaning *life*). The study of all living organisms; it includes the subdivisions *botany* (the study of plants) and *zoology* (the study of animals). *Every student in America studies biology, but too few choose to make biology their life's work.*

4. *cardiology* (from the Greek *kardía,* meaning *heart*). The branch of medicine that addresses the diagnosis and treatment of disorders of the heart. *Lowering the incidence of heart attacks among Americans is one of the primary goals of all cardiologists.*

5. *entomology* (from the Greek *entomon*, meaning *insect*). The study of insects. *Too many students fail to consider entomology as a possible career choice, in spite of its many important contributions to medical science.*

6. *etymology* (from the Greek *etumon*, meaning *true sense of a word*). The study of the origins and historical development of words, including the changes that occur in words as they move from one language to another. *Scholars all over the world study the etymology of their own language in order to better understand their cultures.*

7. *geology* (from the Greek *geo*, meaning *earth*). The science that studies the physical history of Earth and its rocks, as well as the geology of other planets. *Examining the geology of Mars is a fascinating new area of work for many young geologists.*

8. *neurology* (from the Greek *neuro*, meaning *nerves*). The study of the diagnosis and treatment of disorders of the nerves and of the nervous system. *Patients who suffer serious spinal cord injuries depend on neurologists to help them regain mobility.*

9. *ornithology* (from the Greek *ornīth*, meaning *birds*). The branch of zoology that studies birds. *Birdwatching, a popular hobby all over the world, is really an amateur branch of ornithology.*

10. *paleontology* (from the Greek *palaios*, meaning *old* or *ancient*). The study of the life forms of prehistoric times, especially the fossils of plants, animals, and other organisms. *Many students fall in love with science when they first study the paleontology of dinosaurs.*

11. *philology* (from the Greek *philología*, meaning *love of learning and literature*). The scientific study of languages, including their historical development and the relationships between various languages. *Philologists help us understand how and why Shakespeare's English in the 1600s sounded somewhat different from our English, and how our definitions of words sometimes differ from his as well.*

12. *psychology* (from the Greek *psykhe*, meaning *spirit* or *soul*). The scientific study of human and animal behavior. *Psychologists seek to understand the hows and whys of our behavior in order to help us feel and work better.*

PRACTICE 1: MATCHING THE FIELD OF SCIENCE WITH ITS SUBJECT MATTER

Draw lines to match each field of science with the subject matter it studies.

Field of Science	Subject Matter
1. cardiology	**a.** the human nervous system
2. entomology	**b.** human and animal behavior
3. astronomy	**c.** origin of words
4. paleontology	**d.** insects
5. neurology	**e.** history of languages
6. geology	**f.** the human heart
7. ornithology	**g.** all living organisms
8. psychology	**h.** prehistoric life forms
9. anthropology	**i.** history of human beings
10. biology	**j.** physical history of Earth
11. etymology	**k.** birds
12. philology	**l.** outer space

PRACTICE 2: RETESTING YOUR VOCABULARY KNOWLEDGE

Are the following sentences using words correctly? Write T if they make an accurate statement and F if they use the boldfaced word incorrectly. Read carefully; there may be tricks in the statements.

1. Dr. Robert Jarvik, an American **cardiologist**, is best known for his contributions to the development of an artificial human heart.

2. Oceanography, the study of birds, has replaced **ornithology** as the proper name for this scientific field.

3. Sigmund Freud is famous as one of the world's most important **psychologists** for his theories about the workings of the human mind.

4. Dinosaurs are among the principal subjects of study for specialists in **paleontology**.

5. Studying words and their histories is the work of scientists in the field of **neurology**.

6. The study of **astronomy** has been an inspiration to scientists, as well as science fiction writers and moviemakers.

7. Studying rocks, volcanoes, and mountaintops is not the work of **geologists**.

8. **Philology**, a very specialized field of language studies, seeks to trace the development of languages.

9. The study of **biology** is the first requirement essential to the medical profession.

10. If you like bugs and you aren't afraid to touch them, and you like the idea of traveling to faraway jungles, you should consider becoming a professional **etymologist**.

11. Becoming an **entomologist** probably won't make you rich, but you will have the satisfaction of knowing that your study of insects is a serious contribution to the world's scientific knowledge.

12. Margaret Mead, one of the most important **anthropologists** of the twentieth century, studied the cultural influences on adolescence in different cultures, and became famous as an advocate of women's rights.

Lesson 18 Words You Should Now Know

anthropology	geology
astronomy	neurology
biology	ornithology
botany	paleontology
cardiology	philology
discipline	psychology
entomology	zoology
etymology	

Extra Word(s) You Learned in this Lesson:

_____

_____

_____

_____

ANSWERS

Practice 1: Matching the Field of Science with Its Subject Matter

1. f
2. d
3. l
4. h
5. a
6. j
7. k
8. b
9. i
10. g
11. c
12. e

Practice 2: Retesting Your Vocabulary Knowledge

1. T
2. F
3. T
4. T
5. F
6. T
7. F
8. T
9. T
10. F
11. T
12. T

you may see the doctor now

*The art of medicine consists in amusing
the patient while nature cures the disease.*
VOLTAIRE (1694–1778)
FRENCH WRITER

This lesson continues with words about science, but this time, the focus is on words associated with medical science.

THE SCIENCE OF MEDICINE is the scientific area most of us come in contact with. We go to the doctor for check-ups, immunizations, and in unfortunate times, when we're ill. And most of us may see more than one doctor, depending on what hurts or what treatment we need. But just a hundred years ago, most people in the United States had only one doctor, the family doctor.

As with other scientific fields, the practice of medicine has become increasingly specialized. Most doctors now become experts in treating specific parts of the body, and in some cases, treat only one type of disease. Think of the last two doctor visits you made; were they to the same doctor? Probably not. You probably went to one doctor for a general check-up, another to have your teeth cleaned, and still another if you wear eyeglasses.

There are some general words that are used more or less interchangeably to describe doctors. For example, most doctors are known as physicians and are addressed as *Doctor*. Physicians who perform surgery are called surgeons.

Here's a list of doctors you may or may not need in your lifetime, but whose specializations add word power to your vocabulary.

WORDS THAT DESCRIBE DIFFERENT MEDICAL SPECIALISTS

1. *audiologist.* A specialist in the study and treatment of hearing, especially hearing defects. *Jim accompanied his grandmother to the audiologist's office so that she would have company when she got her new hearing aid.*

2. *dermatologist.* A specialist in the branch of medicine dealing with skin and its diseases. *Jenny rushed to the dermatologist for help in treating her poison ivy rash.*

3. *internist.* A specialist in the diagnosis and nonsurgical treatment of diseases, especially of adults. *Mr. Dodson invited his internist to visit the class and explain her career path to students interested in the practice of general medicine.*

4. *nurse practitioner.* A registered nurse with a college nursing degree and advanced training that qualifies him or her to perform some duties of a physician. Many medical offices and clinics employ nurse practitioners who handle simple problems and free doctors to work with complicated cases. *Jason became a nurse practitioner in order to fulfill his lifelong dream to help people.*

5. *obstetrician.* A specialist who cares for women during pregnancy and childbirth. *My mother was so grateful to Abigail, her obstetrician, for helping her through her pregnancy that she named me after her.*

6. *oncologist.* A specialist in the study of cancer, including diagnosis, treatment, and prevention. *People who forget to apply sufficient sunscreen may develop skin problems and need to visit an oncologist.*

7. *ophthalmologist.* A specialist who cares for the eye and its diseases, frequently performing eye surgery. (Note the complicated spelling of *ophthalmologist.*) *I visited an ophthalmologist to treat an eye infection I developed on a recent trip to a rainforest.*

8. *optometrist.* A specialist who examines and treats problems with sight, including the prescribing of corrective lenses. *Janet's optometrist encouraged her to choose eyeglass frames she liked; it was essential that she wear her glasses at all times, no matter what color the frames turned out to be.*

9. *orthodontist*. A dental specialist who corrects irregularly aligned teeth; treatment usually involves braces and sometimes oral surgery. *Since getting his braces, Tim saw his orthodontist more often than he saw his grandmother!*

10. *osteopath*. A specialist who focuses on the muscles and bones to promote and preserve health. *The Sandersons chose to go to an osteopath because of the extra training the doctor had received in muscle and bone manipulation.*

11. *pediatrician*. A specialist concerned with the development, care, and diseases of babies and children. *Children are often reluctant to leave their beloved pediatricians and begin seeing an internist once they reach adulthood.*

12. *podiatrist*. A specialist in the care, diagnosis, and treatment of foot problems. *My mother had to spend a lot of time with her podiatrist as a result of too many days wearing very high heels.*

PRACTICE 1: MATCHING THE BODY PROBLEM WITH THE PHYSICIAN WHO CARES FOR IT

Draw lines to match each body problem with the physician who cares for it.

Body Problem	Physician Who Cares for It
1. blurry vision	a. pediatrician
2. crooked teeth	b. podiatrist
3. tetanus shot	c. audiologist
4. pregnant mother	d. internist
5. hearing loss	e. oncologist
6. skin rash	f. obstetrician
7. baby with measles	g. nurse practitioner
8. ingrown toenail	h. orthodontist
9. continuing stomach pain	i. dermatologist
10. fear of cancer	j. optometrist

PRACTICE 2: MEDICAL CROSSWORD PUZZLE

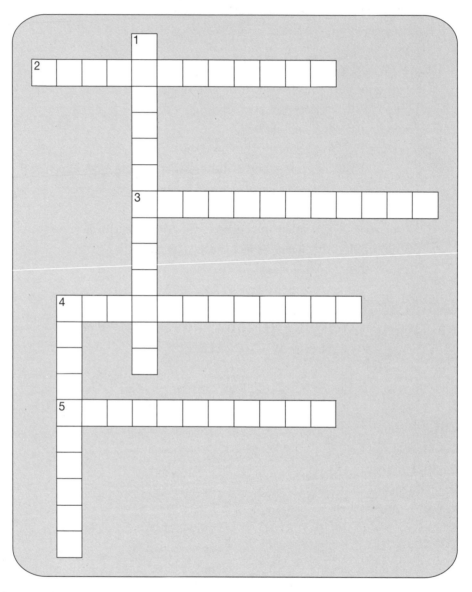

Across
2 doctor who delivers babies
3 doctor who fixes crooked teeth
4 doctor who treats children
5 doctor who provides hearing aids

Down
1 doctor who treats skin problems
4 doctor who treats foot problems

Word Bank
audiologist
dermatologist
obstetrician

orthodontist
pediatrician
podiatrist

Lesson 19 Words You Should Now Know

audiologist	ophthalmologist
dermatologist	optometrist
internist	orthodontist
nurse practitioner	osteopath
obstetrician	pediatrician
oncologist	podiatrist

Extra Word(s) You Learned in This Lesson

_____

_____

_____

_____

ANSWERS

Practice 1: Matching the Body Problem with the Physician Who Cares for It

1. j
2. h
3. g
4. f
5. c
6. i
7. a
8. b
9. d
10. e

ANSWERS

Practice 2: Medical Crossword Puzzle

Across
2 obstetrician
3 orthodontist
4 pediatrician
5 audiologist

Down
1 dermatologist
4 podiatrist

words about families

A family is a unit composed not only of children but of men,
women, an occasional animal, and the common cold.

OGDEN NASH (1902–1971)

AMERICAN HUMORIST

This lesson focuses on words about families, and illustrates many of the complications that arise once we try to define something as simple as *my family*.

HOW MANY PEOPLE are in your family?

Did you include your pets?

Did you count your cousins and aunts and uncles and grandparents?

Are you a member of a blended family?

Have you ever been to a family reunion?

At first glance, we often assume that we know the meaning of a word. For instance, the meaning of the word *family* seems pretty straightforward. But if you hesitated before answering any of the questions above, you know that defining a simple word like *family* isn't easy!

Don't most people assume that a family is the people we live with? But what about grandparents, who usually don't live with us? And what about cousins, who may live across the country or even on another continent? And what about distant relatives we've never met but whose connection to us can be traced by bloodlines? And what if we're the children of divorced and remarried parents? Suddenly, definitions are not so simple.

Anthropologists have devoted decades to studying various cultures and the many ways they define family relationships. For example, in China, there are different words for older brother and younger brother. But in traditional Hawaiian families, there are only two categories: parent and child. Thus, a child refers to all the females of the parents' generation as *mother* and all the males as *father*. All brothers and male cousins are called *brother*, and all sisters and female cousins are known as *sister*. Furthermore, in many Spanish-speaking families, the word *mama* is used to describe any female, regardless of the family relationship.

Following is a list of words referring to families and their various relationships. Knowing these words will definitely increase your word power, and may help you think about your own family in new and interesting ways.

WORDS ABOUT FAMILIES

1. *ancestor*. A person from whom one is descended, especially if more remote than a grandparent. *Our ancestors who lived two or three generations ago were much smaller in both height and weight, as were those who lived millions of years before.*

2. *descendant*. A person, animal, or plant that comes from a specific ancestor. We can even use the word in relation to nonliving things. *The automobile is the descendant of the horse-and-buggy.*

3. *dynasty*. A sequence of rulers from the same family, such as the Ming Dynasty in Chinese history, or a family notable for a particular quality, such as wealth. *The Adams family, which contributed two presidents and several important authors to our country, can surely be termed a true American dynasty.*

4. *family tree*. A chart showing the ancestry, descent, and relationship of all members of a family. *Our family tree proves the theory of genetics: way more than half of us have red hair and green eyes.*

5. *genealogy*. A record of the descent of a person, family, or group from an ancestor or ancestors; or the study of family histories. *The Internet has provided a useful tool for individuals seeking to investigate their genealogical roots.*

6. *generation*. Generally, the entire number of people born and living at about the same time; technically, the period of 30 years accepted as the average between the birth of parents and the birth of their offspring. *People call those born between 1965 and 1976 Generation X; is there a name for your generation yet?*

7. *kin.* A group of people descended from a common ancestor or constituting a family, clan, tribe, or race; relatives collectively are called *kinfolk. Gathering all her kin to her side, my great-grandmother told us the story of her arrival in America.*

8. *monogamy.* Marriage to only one person at a time. *Monogamy is not the only option; some cultures approve other ways of how marriages should be formed.*

9. *nuclear family.* A family unit consisting of a mother, a father, and their children. *A nuclear family of a mother, a father, and two kids is an idealized version of family life we often see on TV shows.*

10. *pedigree.* An ancestral line of descent or ancestry. *Our puppy's pedigree was a mystery: she had ears like a beagle and long legs like a Great Dane!*

11. *polygamy.* The practice of having more than one spouse at a time, also called plural marriage. *Although polygamy is illegal in America, it is still practiced quietly in some areas.*

12. *sibling.* One of two or more individuals with a common parent; a brother or sister. *My older brother accuses me of sibling rivalry because he's allowed to stay out later than I am.*

PRACTICE 1: KNOWING YOUR FAMILY WORDS

Circle the answer that *best* completes each sentence:

1. *Genealogy* is
   a. the entire number of a people in a generation.
   b. the study of family histories.
   c. the descendants of one family.
   d. the total number of one's kin.

2. A *family tree* is
   a. a family that has many branches.
   b. a pedigree of an individual.
   c. a chart showing a family's relationships.
   d. a family's financial records.

3. The Ford family of Detroit is
   a. a famous American dynasty.
   b. an example of a polygamous family.
   c. not at all connected to the car company.
   d. a small kinship group.

4. An individual's *descendants* are
   a. his wife and their children.
   b. his extended family.
   c. his siblings.
   d. his children and grandchildren.

5. One's *ancestors* are
   a. one's brothers and sisters.
   b. one's extended family.
   c. the close relatives who lived before.
   d. one's immediate relatives.

6. A group of persons descended from a common ancestor is called
   a. a descendant.
   b. a family.
   c. a dynasty.
   d. kin.

7. A line of descent tracing ancestry is often called
   a. a pedigree.
   b. a kin group.
   c. a dynasty.
   d. a family.

8. A *nuclear family* is defined as
   a. a family with all its cousins and aunts and uncles.
   b. a mother, a father, and their children.
   c. a monogamous marriage with no children.
   d. a family with more than three children.

9. *Polygamy* is the practice of
   a. marrying in late adolescence.
   b. marrying in early adolescence.
   c. marrying more than one spouse.
   d. marrying in a civil ceremony.

10. A new *generation* appears, on average,
    a. every 30 years.
    b. every 100 years.
    c. every 50 years.
    d. once each century.

PRACTICE 2: RETESTING YOUR KNOWLEDGE

Do the following sentences use this lesson's words correctly? Write T if the boldfaced word is used correctly and F if it is not. Read carefully; there may be tricks in the statements.

_____ 1. A *kin* group is a group of persons descended from a common ancestor.

_____ 2. The *nuclear family* usually contains two children.

_____ 3. The study of *genealogy* is the exclusive work of anthropologists.

_____ 4. A family that contributes great wealth to its community might be called a *dynasty*.

_____ 5. *Monogamy* is the most common form of marriage in most European countries.

_____ 6. Your *family tree* is a description of your parents and your siblings.

_____ 7. A *pedigree* is a record of an ancestral line of descent.

_____ 8. *Sibling* rivalry is the name given to jealousy and competitiveness between sisters and brothers.

_____ 9. *Polygamy* is illegal in the United States.

_____ 10. A *descendant* is a person born into the previous generation.

Lesson 20 Words You Should Now Know

ancestor	kinfolk
descendant	monogamy
dynasty	nuclear family
family tree	pedigree
genealogy	polygamy
generation	sibling
kin	

Extra Word(s) You Learned in this Lesson

_____

_____

_____

_____

_____

_____

_____

_____

ANSWERS

Practice 1: Knowing Your Family Words

1. b
2. c
3. a
4. d
5. c
6. d
7. a
8. b
9. c
10. a

Practice 2: Retesting Your Knowledge

1. T
2. F
3. F
4. T
5. T
6. F
7. T
8. T
9. T
10. F

mind your manners

Manners easily and rapidly mature into morals.
HORACE MANN (1796–1859)
U.S. EDUCATOR AND FIRST GREAT AMERICAN ADVOCATE OF PUBLIC EDUCATION

This lesson focuses on words related to manners—the social rules we use, especially when we're on our best behavior.

EVERY SOCIETY HAS a code of mostly unwritten rules about what constitutes good manners. The rules reflect the society's ideas of how people ought to interact so that they show respect and consideration of one another and communicate effectively. Along the way, the rules are adapted to current situations in a culture. For example, in eighteenth-century European cities, men were expected to walk on the outside of the sidewalk when walking with a lady. The reason: to protect her from flying garbage that was dumped from upstairs windows. This rule acknowledged the current social conditions—there was no citywide garbage service in those days—and suggested the proper manner for gallant men to protect the ladies.

In seventeenth-century France, a country associated with elegance and fine taste, it was still considered perfectly acceptable, even at the royal court, to eat with the hands. In our society, eating with your hands is universally unacceptable, except when eating certain finger foods, such as French fries or chips and dips. However, in many cultures of the Middle East and Africa, eating with the hands is still considered perfectly acceptable behavior. Likewise, in China, it's considered bad manners to give someone a clock; such a gift could be interpreted to mean that the gift-giver was starting a countdown to the recipient's death. And yet in frontier America, to have a clock was a sign of culture and good manners, and to this day clocks are considered an appropriate wedding gift.

Knowing the rules of good manners isn't always automatic, and every child experiences some frustration while learning the rules. Following are some words associated with our society's code of manners. As you learn these words and the rules they represent, think about why they exist and what ideals of behavior they represent in our culture.

WORDS THAT DESCRIBE GOOD MANNERS

1. *cell-phone manners.* The appropriate behavior while using a cell phone; unwritten, yet increasingly common rules of cell-phone behavior such as no loud or humorous ringtones; no cell-phone use in movie theaters, libraries, churches, or schools; and no loud talking. *Can you think of other examples you've seen of good or bad cell-phone manners?*

2. *condolences.* An expression of sympathy for a person who's suffering sorrow, misfortune, or grief; good manners require that handwritten notes of condolence be sent to a grieving person. *When my grandmother died, it was comforting to receive a note of condolence from my teacher.*

3. *etiquette.* The unwritten rules of socially acceptable behavior; the word *etiquette* dates back to eighteenth-century France. *My mother often reminds us that good etiquette is a sign of a good person.*

4. *euphemism.* The substitution of a mild, indirect, or vague expression for one thought to be offensive, harsh, or blunt; for example, when writing a condolence, it may be best to refer to a friend's loss rather than to use the word *death. In America, our euphemism for the word* died *is often a phrase like* passed on *or* passed away.

5. *flag display.* Federal laws, U.S. Code Title 4 Chapter 1, state the rules of etiquette for flying the U.S. flag. *The flag display code requires flying the flag at half-staff for 30 days after the death of a president and ten days after the death of a vice president.*

6. *introductions.* The formal presentation of one person to another or others. In most informal situations, treat both strangers as equals. For example: *"Chris, I'd like you to meet my neighbor Pat."* In more formal situations, introduce strangers more carefully, taking into consideration each person's age and rank, or standing in society. For example: *"Senator Smith, may I present my friend Pat Reid."*

7. *manners.* The socially acceptable way of acting. *"There's really no substitute for good manners," commented Ms. Prim, our homeroom teacher.*

8. *netiquette.* The rules of etiquette, or good manners, that have come to be acceptable during Internet ("net") communication. *It's considered bad netiquette to write emails or post on blogs using ALL CAPITAL LETTERS.*

9. *place cards.* Small cards placed on formal dining tables to designate where each guest should sit. *Place cards are most commonly used at formal events, but they can be very useful for separating screaming children or warring cousins at family holiday gatherings!*

10. *respect.* In every society, respect for others, particularly for the elders of the community, forms the basis for all social customs and rules. *Our grandparents always sit at the head of the table, with the grandchildren spread out around them; it's our way of showing respect for our grandparents.*

11. *RSVP.* The initials of a French phrase, *répondez, s'il vous plaît*, which means *please reply*. These letters appear on invitations, asking the invitee to respond and accept or decline the invitation; sometimes used as a verb. *Don't forget to RSVP so I'll know if you're coming to the party or not!*

12. *thank-you note.* A letter or note written to thank someone for a gift or hospitality. *Sending a thank-you note to my grandmother for the birthday gift she sent me didn't take much time and she said she was pleasantly surprised by my good manners!*

TIP: Every time you witness someone not using good manners, think about why a particular rule of etiquette exists. Knowing the origin of a rule often makes it easier for you to remember to follow it.

PRACTICE 1: DEFINING GOOD MANNERS IN SENTENCES

Fill in the blanks with words you've learned in this lesson.

1. Seating his father at the head of the table, my father observed the custom of _____.

2. Using smiley faces and other emoticons has become an acceptable, if informal, example of _____.

3. Stefanie always decorated her dinner party tables with handwritten _____.

4. After a funeral, you can prove your good manners by sending a note of _____.

5. At funerals for fallen soldiers, the military always observes the formal rules of _____.

6. When you substitute a mild word for a harsh word, you're using a _____.

7. After getting a birthday gift, you'll exhibit good manners and proper etiquette if you write a _____.

8. If you're invited to a wedding or other formal event, you're obligated to send an _____.

9. To show good _____, be brief and direct when you leave a phone message; long messages are rarely welcomed.

10. The rules of _____ may seem silly at first, but once you understand their purpose, to respect others and establish communication within a community, you find them useful and worth observing.

PRACTICE 2: GOOD MANNERS CROSSWORD PUZZLE

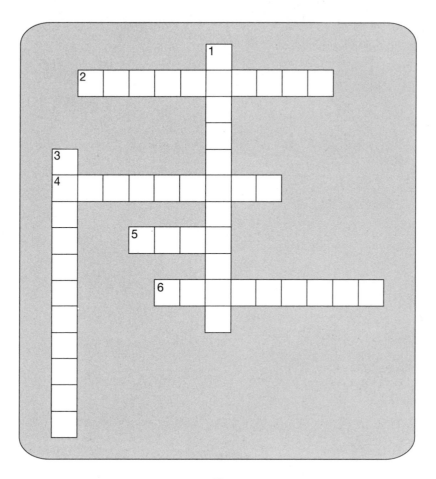

Across

2 expression of comfort to someone grieving

4 softer word for a harsh one

5 response to an invitation

6 dinner table signpost

Down

1 rules for honoring the country's cloth symbol

3 good manners on the Internet

Word Bank

condolence

euphemism

flag display

netiquette

place card

RSVP

Lesson 21 Words You Should Now Know

cell-phone manners	manners
condolences	netiquette
etiquette	place cards
euphemism	respect
flag display	RSVP
introductions	thank-you note

Extra Word(s) You Learned in this Lesson

_____

_____

_____

_____

ANSWERS

Practice 1: Defining Good Manners in Sentences

1. respect for elders
2. netiquette
3. place cards
4. condolence
5. flag display
6. euphemism
7. thank-you note
8. RSVP
9. cell-phone etiquette
10. etiquette

Practice 2: Good Manners Crossword Puzzle

Across
2 condolence
4 euphemism
5 RSVP
6 place card

Down
1 flag display
3 netiquette

words from popular culture

We use the word "hope" perhaps more often than any other word
in the vocabulary: "I hope it's a nice day." "Hopefully, you're
doing well." "So how are things going along? Pretty good.
Going to be good tomorrow? Hope so."

STUDS TERKEL (1912–   )
AMERICAN HISTORIAN AND JOURNALIST

In this lesson, you'll focus on words from the world of popular, or "pop,"
culture—a general pool of ideas and words informally shared by the public.

CERTAIN WORDS, IDEAS, attitudes, and beliefs show up in our lives and
become, from time to time, popular. Their wide acceptance seems to happen
all at once and without any particular explanation. Suddenly, everyone seems
to be thinking the same way, doing the same thing, and using the same
words. When this happens, when something's accepted as interesting, fun, or
fashionable by a lot of people, it becomes part of what we call *popular culture*.

There's also what's called *high culture*. It's that collection of arts (literature, opera, philosophy, and so on) that we commonly associate with highly
educated, cultured people. For example, Shakespeare's plays, Mozart's
music, and museum objects, like the Pharaohs' tombs, are considered high
culture. But popular culture has its art collection, too. Harry Potter's adven-
tures are part of popular culture, as are those of Indiana Jones, a curious
archaeologist who seeks to discover the secrets of past civilizations.

Popular culture is ever-changing, and new fads keep coming and going
at a rapid rate. It doesn't take long for a new idea to become a worldwide
idea, as information is widely distributed and transmitted over the Internet.

Most often, new fads in popular culture don't create entirely new words; they use existing, familiar words in a different way to describe what everyone's doing or talking about. When an individual or only a few people do something, or wear something, no one really notices. But when more and more people follow that lead, the pattern becomes a fad, and as its use becomes even more widespread, we call it a *trend*. Thus, popular culture is formed by the popularization of various trends in every area of life.

Here, you'll find some words that describe current trends or *phenomena* (noteworthy events or facts) in popular culture. None of these were part of the popular culture 25 years ago, when your parents were your age—the elements of pop culture tend to come and go fairly quickly. As you read this list, write down other current pop culture ideas and trends you've noticed.

WORDS THAT DESCRIBE POP CULTURE TRENDS

1. *anime*. This is the Japanese word for animation and has become the word to describe all animation done in the Japanese style, used widely in comic books, video games, and commercials. The comic book store I go to carries a wide selection of anime, which is great because they have become my favorite books to collect.
2. *BFF*. An abbreviation commonly used in text messaging or instant-message chatting to describe a person's *best friend forever. Yesterday I went to the mall with my BFF, Shelly.*
3. *Craigslist*. A network of local communities featuring (mostly) free classified ads in a variety of categories; begun in 1995 by software engineer Craig Newmark, the business is now the single largest classified ad carrier in the world, servicing over 50 countries. *I sold my old bike and bought a new, cooler one on Craigslist, and my parents were proud of my ability to handle both transactions all on my own; I only needed them to provide the money!*
4. *geocaching* (pronounced GEE-oh-cashing). A treasure-hunt game in which players search for caches (or boxes), which usually contain logbooks where players record their names. Players place a cache somewhere, tell players worldwide via the Internet the location using latitude and longitude coordinates. Players then use a GPS device (global positioning system) to find the cache. The fun is in the finding; rarely are there any real treasures to be found. *My parents are enthusiastic geocachers, and we go out hunting at least one weekend a month.*

5. *manga.* The Japanese word for comic books, printed primarily in black and white; English translations are now very collectible. *My dad used to laugh at my collection of manga, but he is now a fan as well.*

6. *multitasking.* The common practice of doing more than one thing at a time. *My brother prides himself on being a first-class multitasker: he can talk on the phone, send text messages, and do his homework, all at the same time.*

7. *organic.* Plants and animals grown and raised without the use of drugs, hormones, or synthetic chemicals. Organic food has come to be an ideal requirement of people seeking to live in a healthy and ethical way. *Being a vegetarian is not enough for my sister; she insists on eating only vegetables grown organically, and she will no longer touch ice cream, formerly her favorite food.*

8. *road rage.* Aggressive and sometimes violent behavior by drivers who are annoyed by other drivers' behavior; the term was first used in 1984 and has become an internationally accepted idea. *The argument between two drivers in the parking lot of our supermarket was the result of road rage, and it ended with one driver in the hospital and the other in jail.*

9. *shout-out.* An acknowledgment or greeting given during a radio or TV show, often to acknowledge fans or family. *It was so cool when my aunt Jane gave me a shout-out during her appearance on a game show!*

10. *speed dating.* A matchmaking process in which people meet for brief (7–8 minutes) conversations, then move on to another person. *Jason's older sister met her husband at a speed-dating event, and she claims he's the best discovery she ever made.*

11. *sudoku.* A number puzzle in which the player must fill a grid of nine squares with numbers; invented by an American in 1979, the puzzle didn't become widely popular until after its success in Japan. *Fans of sudoku, like my math teacher, believe that playing sudoku sharpens the mind.*

12. *texting.* Typing and sending messages via cell phones or other mobile devices. *My parents claim they'd have better conversations with me at dinner if we communicated by texting instead of speaking.*

PRACTICE 1: POPULAR CULTURE WORD SEARCH

Find and circle the words from this lesson in the word search puzzle below.
Words may appear backwards, vertically, or horizontally.

```
N  P  U  H  G  G  O  W  N  E  A  S  R  C  C
A  S  U  C  B  N  G  G  O  B  H  B  O  R  D
L  D  G  H  T  K  I  N  K  O  P  H  A  C  R
Y  G  M  Q  W  X  J  T  U  L  J  Q  D  S  B
B  F  F  G  G  A  S  T  X  N  T  T  R  A  I
A  N  I  M  E  R  O  U  Q  E  Z  R  A  B  O
D  M  B  K  D  U  A  K  V  C  T  G  G  O  D
R  K  V  I  T  A  H  O  C  E  R  T  E  A  Q
K  D  E  Q  G  B  L  D  I  Z  Y  E  I  T  M
E  F  V  N  Q  C  B  U  O  S  D  M  D  A  A
V  C  A  B  R  O  A  S  B  P  F  E  Q  A  V
I  M  T  J  B  T  A  Y  L  O  K  K  H  N  R
R  O  O  K  F  V  K  J  K  V  R  N  F  Y  V
A  D  A  I  K  L  Z  E  D  T  S  C  F  D  Z
K  C  H  K  W  V  F  R  X  H  D  D  D  C  K
```

Word Bank

anime   shout-out

BFF   sudoku

manga   texting

road rage

PRACTICE 2: IDENTIFYING POPULAR CULTURE TRENDS

List three pop-culture ideas, fashions, or customs you've noticed. Then, write
a sentence for each to illustrate the meaning for a reader who might not know
about the trend.

1. _____

2. _____

3. _____

Lesson 22 Words You Should Now Know

anime

BFF

Craigslist

geocaching

manga

multitasking

organic

phenomena

road rage

shout-out

speed dating

sudoku

texting

Extra Word(s) You Learned in This Lesson

_____

_____

_____

_____

ANSWERS

Practice 1: Popular Culture Word Search Solution

```
N  P  U  H  G  G  O  W  N  E  A  S  R  C  C
A  S  U  C  B  N  G  G  O  B  H  B  O  R  D
L  D  G  H  T  K  I  N  K  O  P  H  A  C  R
Y  G  M  Q  W  X  J  T  U  L  J  Q  D  S  B
B  F  F  G  G  A  S  T  X  N  T  T  R  A  I
A  N  I  M  E  R  O  U  Q  E  Z  R  A  B  O
D  M  B  K  D  U  A  K  V  C  T  G  G  O  D
R  K  V  I  T  A  H  O  C  E  R  T  E  A  Q
K  D  E  Q  G  B  L  D  I  Z  Y  E  I  T  M
E  F  V  N  Q  C  B  U  O  S  D  M  D  A  A
V  C  A  B  R  O  A  S  B  P  F  E  Q  A  V
I  M  T  J  B  T  A  Y  L  O  K  K  H  N  R
R  O  O  K  F  V  K  J  K  V  R  N  F  Y  V
A  D  A  I  K  L  Z  E  D  T  S  C  F  D  Z
K  C  H  K  W  V  F  R  X  H  D  D  D  C  K
```

words from the sports arena

One man practicing sportsmanship is
better than a hundred teaching it.
KNUTE ROCKNE (1888–1931)
LEGENDARY FOOTBALL COACH

This lesson focuses on words from the world of sports, many of which are used both on and off the playing field.

IT'S OFTEN SAID that the language of sports is universal. Every city and village has its favorite team; every nation has its favorite sport; and international competitions, like the Olympics, are extraordinarily popular the world over.

In addition to a sense of community pride that cheering for a team promotes, perhaps the best reason sports are so popular is that fans of all ages can imagine themselves right there on the field with their team—playing hard, suffering possible defeat, basking in the glory of a game won in the final, exciting moments. Because both amateurs and professionals play the same games, fans identify with and cheer on their sports heroes, knowing only too well how much effort it takes to give your all repeatedly for the sake of the sport.

Everyone likes the thrill of competing, even if it's only against ourselves, trying to do better this time than last. Watching skilled professionals play, we may wonder how we'd do in their situation. We'd love to do what they do, but in most cases we know we can't. Still, as we watch, we compare individual players to each other and compare their performances to what we know we are capable of doing. If they're well-paid pros, we obviously expect them to do better than we would!

One of the most interesting things about sports-related words is how many of them are applicable in other parts of our lives. Here, you'll find many sports words used every day in other arenas. (Note that *arena* can be defined as a sports field and as a place where events unfold). When we use sports words to describe other ideas, we're using them as metaphors. As you read the list, note how often the words work off the field as well as on. Write down other sports words that come to mind, and be sure to look them up in a dictionary if you're not sure about their exact meanings.

TIP: A *metaphor* is a word or phrase used to describe similarity between two things without using *like* or *as*. For example, *Tom is a tiger on the field* suggests that Tom is fast and ferocious, like a tiger.

WORDS FROM THE WORLD OF SPORTS

1. *aerobic.* Something or someone that utilizes oxygen in order to live. *The coach required all his players to do at least one hour a day of aerobic exercises.*
2. *calisthenics.* Gymnastic exercises that are usually performed with little or no special apparatus. *Every morning our homeroom teacher requires us to do five minutes of calisthenics in order to wake us up.*
3. *decathlon.* An athletic contest comprising ten different track-and-field events and won by the contestant amassing the highest total score. (Note the spelling of this word; it is easy to add an extra, unwanted syllable to it and pronounce it de-cath-A-lon, which is incorrect.) *Customarily, men compete more frequently in decathlons than women do, but slowly, that's beginning to change.*
4. *draft.* Outside sports, this word can mean a preliminary drawing or document, such as the first draft of a book; it can also mean a path of air, such as in a chimney. In sports, a draft is the selection of new players by a professional team, from a group of amateur players. *The student council drafted its treasurer to be in charge of purchasing decorations for the Halloween party.*

5. *Ironman.* A triathlon race held once a year in Hawaii that includes an ocean swim, a bike ride, and a marathon foot race. The event takes its name from a comic book character with great athletic endurance. *Our quarterback is a regular ironman when it comes to getting that ball down the field.*

6. *kickoff.* In football and soccer, a kick that puts a stationary ball in motion and begins a period of play. *The candidate announced his campaign with a kickoff speech at the state convention.*

7. *kinetic.* Something produced by motion. *The kinetic energy of the young gymnasts at the Olympics was thrilling to watch.*

8. *marathon.* A long-distance running event of 26 miles and 385 yards named for the story of a messenger's long run in 490 B.C. from the Battle of Marathon to Athens. *The dance marathon lasted more than 24 hours, until the dancers collapsed in exhaustion.*

9. *offsides.* To be illegally beyond an allowed line or area or ahead of the ball in football or soccer. *The candidate's campaign was offsides when it accused her opponent of foul play.*

10. *out of left field.* In baseball, left field is the area in the outfield to the left of a person standing at home plate while facing the pitcher's mound. *When we describe someone or something as coming out of left field, we mean that the person is acting odd or strange, or the event is happening without warning.*

11. *three strikes.* In baseball, a batter strikes out when he or she has struck at or failed to hit three good balls. In legal terms, some laws demand severe punishment after someone has been convicted of three crimes. *The drug dealer, convicted for the third time, was sentenced to 95 years in prison under the three strikes law.*

12. *time-out.* In sports, a brief interruption in play called to make substitutions or discuss strategy, or the like. *My parents try to calm my little sister down by assigning time-outs to her so that the rest of us can have some peace and quiet.*

PRACTICE: SPORTS CROSSWORD PUZZLE

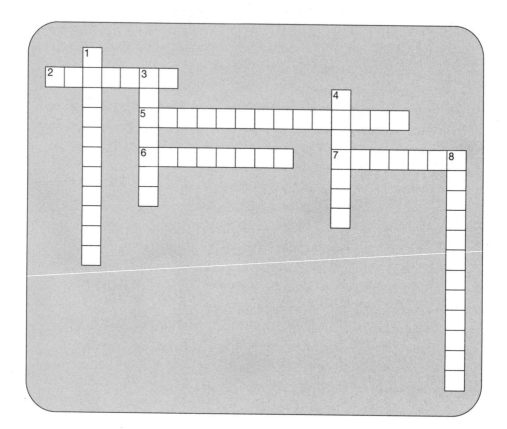

Across

2 exercise that uses oxygen
5 to act odd or strange
6 26+ mile race
7 moving and energetic

Down

1 failure at bat
3 extremely difficult three-part race
4 the beginning of a game or contest
8 exercise without machines or weights

Word Bank

aerobic
calisthenics
Ironman
kickoff

kinetic
marathon
out of left field
three strikes

Lesson 23 Words You Should Now Know

aerobic

calisthenics

decathlon

draft

Ironman

kickoff

kinetic

marathon

metaphor

offsides

out of left field

three strikes

time-out

Extra Word(s) You Learned in this Lesson

_____

_____

_____

_____

ANSWERS

Practice: Sports Crossword Puzzle Solution

Across

2 aerobic

5 out of left field

6 marathon

Down

1 three strikes

3 Ironman

4 kickoff

words about politics

All our work, our whole life is a matter of semantics, because
words are the tools with which we work, the material out of which
laws are made, out of which the Constitution was written.
Everything depends on our understanding of them.
FELIX FRANKFURTER (1882–1965)
ASSOCIATE JUSTICE OF THE UNITED STATES SUPREME COURT

In this lesson, you'll learn words about politics. At first, you may consider yourself too young to care about politics if you are too young to vote. However, as you learn the words in this lesson, you'll see that many of these words are useful in your life right now—in school and at home.

POLITICS. POLITICS. POLITICS. No doubt you've gotten tired of hearing people talk politics enthusiastically, sometimes angrily, and always endlessly. What's the big deal? Well, when you stop to think about it, politics is one of the most important topics anyone can discuss. Even you.

Politics is defined as *the art or science of governing, especially the activities engaged in by a government, politician, or political party.* Simply put, politics is how our country, city, or neighborhood works and what our rights and responsibilities are as citizens. All those details are determined by political decisions within our government.

One of the most famous comments about politics was made by Thomas P. O'Neill, Jr., a long-serving congressman from Massachusetts. He said, *All politics is local.* What he meant is that the big ideas that politicians often talk about aren't what really matters to most people. Instead, the local, right-here-in-our-neighborhood issues are what matter to voters, and therefore should matter to their elected officials.

Even if you're not old enough to vote, are there local issues that matter to you? Are there conditions at your school that you'd like to change? Are local parks open when you and your friends want to use them? Do you wish your neighborhood had a dog park? Do parks need to be cleaned up? These are local issues about which you may have a political opinion.

The following list of words, many used frequently in political conversations, will help you build word power, and maybe even help you influence local political decisions.

WORDS ABOUT POLITICS

1. *caucus.* A meeting organized in support of a particular interest, group, or cause. *Members of the Green Party met in caucus last month to nominate their candidates.*

2. *constituent.* A part of a whole; a resident in a place represented by an elected official. *The congresswoman's constituents demanded that she listen to their complaints.*

3. *facilitate.* To make something happen easily. *When groups disagree, they may need a go-between to facilitate an understanding about the differences between them.*

4. *federal.* The central government of a country. *The federal government oversees the maintenance of the highways that connect all the states.*

5. *hierarchy.* The arrangement of anything, usually people, in order of rank or importance. *The Congress of the United States assigns its members office space based on a hierarchy of seniority; those who have served longest get the nicest offices.*

6. *ideology.* A set of ideas or beliefs that form the basis of a political, economic, or philosophical system. *Our country's ideology demands that we treat all people equally; in practice, we don't always live up to our ideals.*

7. *implement.* As a noun, describes an instrument or tool used to perform an activity; as a verb, describes the act of making something happen. *As a nation, we often fail to implement the goals we set for ourselves.*

8. *incentive.* Something that motivates or encourages someone to do something, often a reward. *During election season, candidates running for office have a strong incentive to please the voters.*

9. *infrastructure.* The basic facilities and services needed for a community or system to function. *We depend on the infrastructure of our city, including clean water, electricity, and streets in good condition.*

10. *legislate.* To pass laws or modify existing laws. *Women in the United States struggled for decades until finally, in 1920, the federal government passed legislation that gave all women the right to vote.*

11. *mediate.* To resolve differences or to bring about a settlement between conflicting parties. *The committee chair often had to mediate between warring groups who refused to modify their opinions.*

12. *protocol.* The customs, regulations, and etiquette that govern a particular situation; or a document or treaty between states. *The proper protocol when being introduced to royalty is to bow or curtsy; when meeting elected officials, one waits for the official to extend his or her hand.*

PRACTICE 1: CHECKING YOUR KNOWLEDGE OF POLITICAL WORDS

Circle the correct meaning for the italicized word in each sentence.

1. *Hierarchy* means
   a. an order of rank.
   b. a group of politicians.
   c. a committee decision.

2. *Federal* is a term for
   a. a vote by the people.
   b. a central governing body.
   c. a savings bank.

3. To *facilitate* is to
   a. vote in an election.
   b. make something happen.
   c. be elected to office.

4. A *constituent* is
   a. a member of a group.
   b. an elected official.
   c. a law about to be voted on.

5. To *implement* is to
   a. submit to a vote.
   b. argue for a position.
   c. make something happen.

6. *Ideology* is
   a. a group's vote.
   b. a set of ideas of beliefs.
   c. a committee proposal.

7. An *incentive* is
   a. something that motivates.
   b. a majority vote.
   c. an elected official.

8. To *mediate* is to
   a. agree on a difficult position.
   b. propose a new law.
   c. resolve differences between two groups.

9. A *caucus* is
   a. a new idea or process.
   b. a majority vote.
   c. a meeting in support of a particular interest.

10. To *legislate* is to
   a. argue local issues.
   b. take a group vote.
   c. pass laws.

PRACTICE 2: USING POLITICAL WORDS IN SENTENCES

Fill in the blanks with words you've learned in this lesson.

1. The committee chairperson offered a/an _____ to the members in order to get them to agree on her proposal.

2. The _____ government of the country oversees the individual states.

3. A senator's _____ is the set of beliefs which determine how she will vote on proposals for new laws.

4. The animal rights group held a town _____ in order to plan the details of their latest campaign.

5. An effective leader is able to _____ his ideas with the support of his constituents.

6. The highways of our country are an important part of its _____.

7. The single most important function of government is to _____ on behalf of the people.

8. Every elected official must listen carefully to the desires of his or her _____.

9. The set of rules or customs by which relations between countries are conducted is called the international _____.

10. The system that decides which individuals in a group are ranked higher or lower is called a _____.

Lesson 24 Words You Should Now Know

caucus	ideology
constituent	infrastructure
facilitate	legislate
federal	mediate
hierarchy	protocol

Extra Word(s) You Learned in This Lesson

_____

_____

_____

_____

ANSWERS

Practice 1: Checking Your Knowledge of Political Words

1. a
2. b
3. b
4. a
5. c
6. b
7. a
8. c
9. c
10. c

Practice 2: Using Political Words in Sentences

1. incentive
2. federal
3. ideology
4. caucus
5. implement
6. infrastructure
7. legislate
8. constituents
9. protocol
10. hierarchy

words about computers

Computers make it easier to do a lot of things, but most of the things they make it easier to do don't need to be done.

ANDY ROONEY (1919–)

AMERICAN HUMORIST

This lesson focuses on words associated with computers, many of which describe things you probably do every day.

YOU'RE TOO YOUNG to remember that far-off historical time before computers existed, although it wasn't really so long ago. Just ask your parents. But you may well remember way back to the day you first sat down at a computer, or better yet, that day when you were first allowed to sit at the computer as long as you wanted and you discovered all the amazing things it could do.

A computer is like a whole universe in a box, a doorway for education, entertainment, and much more. It provides a way for you to communicate with friends, as well as make new ones all over the world. You probably have access to a computer at your school, library, or at home. And you probably know how to do a lot of different computer activities. What you may *not* know are the definitions of some words associated with computers.

Here's a list of computer words whose precise definitions you need to know. The words may describe things you see or activities you perform frequently on the computer, or they may describe ideas and issues about computers of which you're only vaguely aware. As you read the list, write down other computer-connected words that come to mind, and look them up in a dictionary to make sure you really understand them.

WORDS THAT DESCRIBE COMPUTER FUNCTIONS AND ACTIVITIES

1. *browser.* A computer browser is a program on your computer that lets you view, download, and use sites on the Internet. A browser is also a person who explores, as in a library or on the Internet. *I like the browser I've always used to surf the Internet, but my geeky brother wants to switch us to some new one he says downloads ten times faster.*

2. *copyright law.* The law that grants to the author (or other owner of the copyright) the exclusive right to make copies or allow others to make copies of anything created or written, including literary, musical, artistic, audio, or video works. This law applies to almost everything you read on the Internet. For example, you may not copy a newspaper story or an encyclopedia article without getting permission from the author or owner of the article. *The committee discovered that Bill broke the copyright law because he downloaded the story and then claimed that he had written it.*

3. *desktop publishing.* The use of computer software on a personal computer to design and produce publications. *Our student newspaper now looks like a real paper because we use a desktop publishing program.*

4. *domain name.* An Internet address owned by a person or organization to identify the location of its Web pages. Domain suffixes indicate the type of material on the pages: .com for commercial enterprises; .org for nonprofit organizations; .gov for government websites; .edu for educational institutions. *What's the domain name of your school? The website you visit most often?*

5. *icon.* A picture or image that represents something. On a computer, an icon is a picture or symbol for a command, program, or function. *The use of icons to represent words and ideas allows users who speak different languages to understand the same information.*

6. *ISP* (Internet service provider). A company or organization that provides access to the Internet, usually for a fee. Service, as electronic signals, may come from a phone company through telephone wires or a cable company through TV cables. *I saw lots of TV commercials promising better, faster download time, but I don't want to change my Internet service provider.*

7. *search engine.* Computer software that searches the Internet for documents containing a keyword, phrase, or subject you submit. *Many people type their own name into a search engine to see where they appear on the Internet; the results can be surprising.*

8. *social networking.* Websites that enable people to meet and share information. *MySpace.com and Facebook.com are two extremely popular and competitive social networking sites.*

9. *spam.* Unrequested commercial messages usually sent as emails. *Many computer users complain that unwanted spam messages are a frequent and unpleasant interruption.*

10. *streaming.* To stream is to flow, as in a river. As a computer word, streaming refers to the technology that enables the delivery of a steady stream of information or images, such as a streaming video of a live concert. *Viewing streaming video on a computer feels like watching a private showing of a blockbuster film on your own personal movie screen!*

11. *URL* (Uniform Resource Locator). The system used for specifying addresses on the Internet. Each individual file or page has its own URL, which is located on the address bar at the top of your Internet browser window. *Be sure to type the information in a URL carefully so your browser knows where to go.*

12. *World Wide Web* (www). The complete set of electronic documents connected over the Internet. Informally, the terms *Internet, the Web,* and *online* are used interchangeably. Which term do you and your friends use most often? *When you're wandering around the World Wide Web, you can be described as surfing the Web or browsing the Internet.*

PRACTICE 1: MATCHING THE COMPUTER WORD WITH ITS DEFINITION

Draw lines to match each computer word with its definition.

Computer Word	Definition
1. copyright law	**a.** websites for making friends
2. browser	**b.** continuous flow of material over the Internet
3. search engine	**c.** the exclusive ownership of material by an author
4. ISP	**d.** online address
5. icon	**e.** software that looks up websites
6. spam	**f.** the system for finding Web pages
7. URL	**g.** program for accessing Web pages
8. streaming	**h.** unwanted emails
9. domain name	**i.** service that provides Internet access
10. social networking	**j.** image that represents files or functions online

PRACTICE 2: COMPUTER WORDS WORD SEARCH

Find and circle the words from this lesson in the word search puzzle below. Words may appear backwards, vertically, or horizontally.

```
H  S  B  D  N  W  H  V  D  T  G  P  S  I  I
L  R  U  V  V  Z  V  E  E  P  K  M  P  G  X
X  T  U  W  Y  I  D  N  D  I  H  Z  J  D  P
M  H  Y  J  D  M  R  F  S  B  X  T  F  Y  S
F  G  D  K  V  E  W  P  O  B  V  X  I  O  P
N  I  L  O  T  M  A  W  K  O  A  F  R  D  N
M  R  Y  N  M  K  W  K  O  O  K  U  S  T  I
H  Y  I  X  C  A  H  P  M  D  D  P  P  N  L
L  P  I  P  S  J  I  M  L  I  D  M  A  S  A
Z  O  S  X  S  F  H  N  T  Y  R  Q  M  O  C
L  C  T  F  H  O  M  A  F  H  D  Y  I  N  D
H  K  G  J  I  N  S  J  K  I  J  U  D  C  H
N  W  L  V  J  A  Q  U  Z  A  R  I  P  T  Q
T  C  A  S  T  V  X  Q  L  I  Y  P  J  A  L
B  R  O  W  S  E  R  R  X  P  T  A  T  V  G
```

Word Bank

browser	ISP
copyright	spam
domain	URL
Internet	

Lesson 25 Words You Should Now Know

browser	social networking
copyright law	spam
desktop publishing	streaming
domain name	URL
icon	World Wide Web
ISP	
search engine	

Extra Word(s) You Learned in this Lesson

_____

_____

_____

_____

ANSWERS

Practice 1: Match the Computer Word with Its Definition

1. c
2. g
3. e
4. i
5. j
6. h
7. f
8. b
9. d
10. a

Practice 2: Word Search for Computer Words

```
H  S  B  D  N  W  H  V  D  T  G  P  S  I  I
L  R  U  V  V  Z  V  E  E  P  K  M  P  G  X
X  T  U  W  Y  I  D  N  D  I  H  Z  J  D  P
M  H  Y  J  D  M  R  F  S  B  X  T  F  Y  S
F  G  D  K  V  E  W  P  O  B  V  X  I  O  P
N  I  L  O  T  M  A  W  K  O  A  F  R  D  N
M  R  Y  N  M  K  W  K  O  O  K  U  S  T  I
H  Y  I  X  C  A  H  P  M  D  D  P  P  N  L
L  P  I  P  S  J  I  M  L  I  D  M  A  S  A
Z  O  S  X  S  F  H  N  T  Y  R  Q  M  O  C
L  C  T  F  H  O  M  A  F  H  D  Y  I  N  D
H  K  G  J  I  N  S  J  K  I  J  U  D  C  H
N  W  L  V  J  A  Q  U  Z  A  R  I  P  T  Q
T  C  A  S  T  V  X  Q  L  I  Y  P  J  A  L
B  R  O  W  S  E  R  R  X  P  T  A  T  V  G
```

S E C T I O N   4

build word power in special ways

WITH ALL THE NEW KNOWLEDGE you've acquired, you're now ready to fine-tune your vocabulary and show off your word power. The final section of this book shows you ways to use slang, confusing words, foreign phrases, and extra fancy words to beef up your vocabulary and become an extremely powerful wordsmith.

words we've adopted

*We don't just borrow words; on occasion, English has pursued
other languages down alleyways to beat them unconscious
and rifle their pockets for new vocabulary.*
BOOKER T. WASHINGTON (1856–1915)
AMERICAN EDUCATOR

This lesson focuses on words that originated in other languages but are now
common in English.

AS YOU LEARNED in Lesson 6, English is a relatively young language, and
has derived hundreds of thousands of words from older languages, princi-
pally Latin and Greek. (You may want to look back at that lesson for a quick
review!)

When words were borrowed from older languages and moved into English, they were *anglicized*—modified and adapted to English pronunciations
and spellings. As a result, they aren't immediately recognizable as borrow-
ings to anyone but linguists (people who speak several languages fluently);
we think of the words as our own.

There are also many, many words from other, older languages that
moved directly into English. Sometimes the pronunciation is modified
slightly, but for the most part, these words were adopted as is, without signifi-
cant changes. Some words feel so natural to us that it takes a moment to real-
ize that they're technically foreign words. Others keep the pronunciation
from their original language, and are therefore more easily recognized as foreign imports.

Knowing the meaning of many words and how to pronounce them is a sure sign of word power, your goal in reading this book!

Following is a list of words that are direct imports to English. You may already know some of them. Aids to their pronunciations are included to help you if needed.

WORDS FROM FOREIGN SOURCES

1. *ad hoc* (from Latin for *for this*). Something created right now, or improvised, for a specific purpose. *Hurricane Katrina caused the ad hoc formation of citizen rescue teams.*

2. *ad hominem* (add-HOHM-eh-nihm). (from Latin for *to the man*) An argument that attacks someone's character rather than attacking his argument, appealing to the emotions rather than the intellect. *Political races are too often full of ad hominem attacks instead of debates on the real issues.*

3. *camouflage* (KAM-uh-flaahj). (from the French for *to disguise*) Disguising for protection from an enemy, such as dressing to blend into the surrounding environment. *Clothes designed with a camouflage pattern have become popular with young people, whether or not they plan to serve in the military.*

4. *caveat emptor* (KAH-vee-aht em(p)-tor). (from the Latin for *let the buyer beware*) The concept that not all sellers can be trusted, so buyers should carefully judge the quality of what they buy before they pay. *Flea market bargain hunters should remember the saying caveat emptor every time they think they've bought something for much less than it's really worth.*

5. *cocoa*. (the Spanish name for the bean of the cacao tree) The powder ground from roasted cacao beans. *Imagine our world without cocoa: if the Spanish hadn't come to the New World, no one in Europe or Asia would ever have had the pleasure of a cup of cocoa.*

6. *faux pas* (fō-PAH). (from the French for *false step*) An embarrassing mistake in manners or conduct. *I made a terrible faux pas when I commented to my teacher that she seemed to have gained weight over the summer.*

7. *matinee* (ma-tuh-NEH). (from the French for *morning*) An entertainment or performance held in the afternoon. *We were so anxious to see that new comedy that we stood in line for the Saturday matinee.*

8. *objet d'art* (ahb-zjay-DART). (from the French for *object of art*) A work of art, usually small; sometimes simply called objet or (plural) objets. *My aunt owns a gift shop that specializes in antique French objets d'art.*

9. *pirouette* (peer-uh-WET). (from the French for *spinning top*) In ballet, a complete turn of the body on the point of the toe or the ball of the foot. *The ballerina amazed the audience with her ability to do multiple pirouettes in rapid succession.*

10. *pizza* (from the Italian for *bite*). An open-faced baked pie topped usually with spiced tomato sauce, cheese, and other garnishes. *Pizza is thought by many to have originated in the United States, but others point out that an early form of pizza was eaten by the ancient Greeks, who flavored their flat breads with herbs and onions as early as 500 B.C.*

11. *potpourri* (pō-puh-REE). (from the French for *rotten pot*) A mixture of dried flower petals and spices, kept in a jar for their fragrance; also, any mixture of assorted objects. *Jasmine always keeps a vase of potpourri scented with jasmine in her room; for obvious reasons, jasmine is her favorite flower.*

12. *pro bono publico* (prō bōnoh POOH-blē- koh). (from the Latin *for the public good*) Something done for the public good without payment; often shortened to pro bono. *Many lawyers contribute their services pro bono to help those who are unable to pay.*

PRACTICE 1: MATCHING THE FOREIGN-BORN WORD WITH ITS ENGLISH MEANING

Draw lines to match each foreign-born word with its English meaning.

Foreign-Born Word	English Meaning
1. pirouette	a. mixture of dried flowers and spices
2. ad hoc	b. argument attacking a person, not a position
3. faux pas	c. reminder to buyers to be careful
4. matinee	d. ballet step turning on one foot
5. potpourri	e. work done for free
6. ad hominem	f. created on the spot, improvised
7. objet d'art	g. embarrassing use of bad manners
8. caveat emptor	h. a favorite food the world over
9. pro bono	i. afternoon performance
10. pizza	j. small object of artistic value

PRACTICE 2: FOREIGN-BORN WORDS CROSSWORD PUZZLE

Across
2 afternoon performance
3 whirling dance move
4 a bad manners mistake
5 created on the spot

Down
1 designed to deceive
3 fragrant mixture from nature

Word Bank

ad hoc	matinee
camouflage	pirouette
faux pas	potpourri

Lesson 26 Words You Should Now Know

ad hoc	matinee
ad hominem	objet d'art
camouflage	pirouette
caveat emptor	pizza
cocoa	potpourri
faux pas	pro bono publico
linguist	

Extra Word(s) You Learned in this Lesson

_____

_____

_____

_____

ANSWERS

Practice 1: Matching the Foreign-Born Word with Its English Meaning

1. d
2. f
3. g
4. i
5. a
6. b
7. j
8. c
9. e
10. h

Practice 2: Foreign-Born Words Crossword Puzzle

Across
2 matinee
3 pirouette
4 faux pas
5 ad hoc

Down
1 camouflage
3 potpourri

words that really
mean something else

The great enemy of clear language is insincerity. When there is a gap between one's real and one's declared aims, one turns as it were instinctively to long words and exhausted idioms, like a cuttlefish squirting out ink.

GEORGE ORWELL (1903–1950)

BRITISH ESSAYIST AND NOVELIST

This lesson focuses on euphemisms, words that we use to avoid using other words.

AS YOU LEARNED in Lesson 21, a *euphemism* is a substitution of a mild, indirect, or vague expression for one that might be thought offensive, harsh, or too blunt. This might suggest that speakers and writers use euphemisms merely to display good manners, but euphemisms are used for other reasons, not all of which are honest attempts to be more polite or avoid offending anyone.

Euphemisms are often used

- to avoid speaking directly about something one fears,
- to avoid speaking the truth; using double talk to hide one's real meaning,
- to avoid naming a person or thing, using a synonym in order to appear innocent of slander,

- to avoid naming something considered taboo (unacceptable, forbidden in polite society),
- to avoid repeating the same name or idea, as a name-calling device in political or social issue debates,
- to avoid revealing a secret or allowing others to overhear a name (frequently used in spy novels and movies),
- to avoid too much seriousness and make light of a difficult situation.

HOW WILL EUPHEMISMS BUILD YOUR WORD POWER?

As you know, the best way to increase your vocabulary is to read—this book and anything and everything else! Additionally, listen carefully to everything you hear—on the radio and TV, in conversations with friends, parents, and teachers. You'll pick up lots of new words to help increase your vocabulary. You'll soon be acquiring new words unconsciously, without using flash cards or study lists or even thinking about it!

Listening for euphemisms also increases your vocabulary and your sensitivity to word meanings. As you notice euphemisms, you'll automatically sense the variations and nuances (small differences in meaning) in language that euphemisms employ. For example, if someone says they live in a *working class neighborhood*, you may guess that they don't live in the wealthiest, fanciest part of town. When someone says a neighborhood is *in transition*, what do you think they mean? What reality does the euphemism cover?

TIP: How do you know if a word or phrase is a euphemism or simply a synonym? Ask yourself what the motive was for choosing the word or words. Why this particular word? Does it hide some secret motive? If the answer is yes, then it's probably a euphemism.

Euphemisms aren't usually made up of difficult words, but are usually a sign that a sensitive or complicated idea is being simplified or covered up. The following is a list of some common euphemisms. As you read the list, write down other euphemisms you've heard.

EUPHEMISMS ABOUT DEATH

This is the largest category of frequently used euphemisms, no doubt because death is so universally feared and so little understood.

Examples
passed away; checked out; bit the Big One; kicked the bucket; bought the farm; pushing daisies; sleeping the Big Sleep; gone six feet under

Notice how all these phrases include a hint of humor to mask the seriousness of the subject they are refusing to acknowledge directly.

EUPHEMISMS ABOUT POLITICS

Next to death, the subject that probably causes the most emotion—and therefore prompts the frequent use of euphemisms—is politics. Have you heard politicians use any of these euphemisms, and can you describe what they actually mean?

Examples
free the people; tax the rich and give to the poor; reclaim our cities; shake up Washington; loosen government controls; stop big government

EUPHEMISMS ABOUT WAR

The terrible circumstances of war create numerous opportunities for speakers and writers to attempt to soften the blow of war's harsh realities.

Examples
friendly fire (accidental killing of one's own comrades); collateral damage (killing innocent bystanders); pacification (killing or controlling citizens of enemy states); post-traumatic stress disorder, also referred to as PTSD (emotional and mental disturbances resulting from war experiences)

EUPHEMISMS ABOUT EDUCATION

The educational system creates more than its share of euphemisms by seeking to paint a pretty picture (another euphemism) to address difficult problems.

> **Examples**
> social promotion (advancing a failing student to the next grade even if his or her academic performance is not adequate); holding back (failing a student a whole grade year); English Language Learners (the latest term for people learning English as a second language); special ed (education for students who have difficulty in regular classes); No Child Left Behind (the policy of testing student and school performance against national standards to detect inadequate educational performance)

> **TIP:** Listen and read carefully. When you catch a euphemism being used, try to translate it into the reality it's seeking to mask.

PRACTICE: UNMASKING EUPHEMISMS

Rewrite the following sentences, replacing the italicized euphemism with more direct language. Briefly explain why you think the euphemism was used.

1. Because of budget cuts at the company, my mother's job was *terminated without prejudice.*

_____

2. Sadly, the neighborhood where we used to live is now said to be *in transition.*

_____

3. To her great embarrassment, Eileen's mother called her *pleasingly plump.*

_____

4. Moe's *Pre-Owned Vehicles* was the newest business in town, and apparently it was extremely successful in these hard financial times.

_____

5. Every Tuesday night we put out our recycling bins for the *sanitation engineers* to pick up on Wednesday mornings.

_____

6. The general explained that many civilian casualties resulted during the platoon's efforts to *neutralize the target*.

_____

7. Mary Lou was *expecting* again, which pleased her son and her parents enormously.

_____

8. During this summer's heat wave we suddenly had no electricity in my apartment, and the whole city experienced a *disruption in service*.

_____

9. According to his defense attorney, the accused robber's statement in court was *not completely true*.

10. The town instituted the use of school buses to enforce its new commitment to a policy of *diversity*.

_____

Lesson 27 Words You Should Now Know

collateral damage	pacification
English Language Learners	post-traumatic stress disorder
friendly fire	social promotion
holding back	special ed
No Child Left Behind	taboo

Extra Word(s) You Learned in This Lesson

_____

_____

_____

_____

ANSWERS

Practice: Unmasking Euphemisms

1. Because of budget cuts at the company, my mother's job was *eliminated*.
   The writer wanted to make it clear that the mother was not to blame for the loss of her job.

2. Sadly, the neighborhood where we used to live is now said to be *a less desirable place to live*.
   The writer is trying not to say that different kinds of people are moving in, probably causing property values to decline.

3. To her great embarrassment, Eileen's mother called her *slightly overweight*.
   Probably Eileen's mother thinks her daughter is more than slightly overweight and actually fat, but is trying to soften the blow by calling her pleasingly plump; the mother is hardly pleased and is trying to cover her displeasure with a bit of humor.

4. Moe's *Used Cars* was the newest business in town, and apparently it was extremely successful in these hard financial times.
   Calling used cars *pre-owned* is an attempt to make them sound more desirable, since used cars are generally thought to be of little value.

5. Every Tuesday night we put out our recycling bins for the *garbage men* to pick up on Wednesday mornings.
   Calling garbage men sanitation engineers is an attempt to make this difficult and distasteful job sound more respectable and somehow scientific and skilled.

6. The general explained that many civilian casualties resulted during the platoon's efforts to *defeat the enemy forces*.
   Neutralizing the target is a dramatically deceptive and euphemistic way to describe the cold hard facts of war. Presumably it is an attempt by military spokespersons to protect the feelings of civilians.

7. Mary Lou was *pregnant* again, which pleased her son and her parents enormously.
   Strangely, the word *pregnant* continues to be considered slightly taboo. In centuries past, in many middle- and upper-class circles, women went into seclusion and never appeared in public during pregnancy.

8. During this summer's heat wave we suddenly had no electricity in my apartment, and the whole city experienced a *power outage.*

A power outage, also known as a *blackout,* is often referred to by power companies as a disruption in service to appease the possibility of panic. The term power outage gives little hint of when the power might return and in fact, it sounds as if the power will be out indefinitely. On the other hand, a *disruption* in service implies the power is only out temporarily— something has gotten in the way of its service, but that the disruption will be fixed soon.

9. According to his defense attorney, the accused robber's statement in court was *at least false in part.*

The defense attorney is trying to mask the fact that his client misrepresented at least part of the truth. Including the word *true* in the phrase *not completely true* is an attempt to suggest that at least part of the statement was not a lie.

10. The town instituted the use of school buses to enforce its new commitment to a policy of *ensuring that the student bodies of its schools included students of all races.*

Racial inequality remains one of the most controversial and emotional issues in American life. The euphemistic word *diversity* is used as shorthand whenever speakers are referring to the issue of inequality among the races.

LESSON 28

confused and abused words

First learn the meaning of what you say, and then speak.
EPICTETUS (CA. 55–CA. 135)
GREEK PHILOSOPHER

This lesson focuses on two categories of words: those frequently confused and those frequently abused.

BY NOW, YOU might be feeling overloaded with new words, and even a bit hesitant to use any words you already know. Learning new vocabulary is intense work. This lesson provides a break by concentrating on two common vocabulary problems.

1. Confused words. The English language is full of confusing word pairs—they sound similar but mean different things. How can you avoid being confused? Find out here.

2. Abused words. Because it has inherited words from dozens of other languages, English is probably the richest language in the world. So why do we keep on using the same old words over and over again? Here you'll find out which words you probably use way too often.

WORDS THAT CONFUSE

Following is a list of some word pairs that are frequently confused. Pay close attention to the sample sentences in which they're used. Seeing a word used properly can help you acquire it for your own vocabulary.

1. *adopt.* To accept as one's own.
   adapt. To adjust to or become accustomed to; to modify.
   > My family decided to adopt a puppy to be a companion to our old dog.
   > The puppy adapted to our family very easily; she loved all the other animals.

2. *all together.* A group of things or persons gathered together.
   altogether. Entirely, completely.
   > Our pets, all together, resemble a very zany zoo.
   > My mom is not altogether in agreement that we should now get an ostrich.

3. *complement.* Something that is added in, that contributes.
   compliment. A remark that pleases or flatters someone.
   > The new puppy complemented our collection of both old and young pets.
   > The veterinarian complimented us on our amazing menagerie of pets.

4. *continuous.* Occurring without interruption.
   continual. Happening repeatedly, over and over again.
   > The pets provide continuous joy to all of us; they are so sweet and loving.
   > Trips to the vet are a continual problem; one of the animals always needs care.

5. *everyone.* A pronoun that describes a group; everybody in the group.
   every one. The specific individuals in a group.
   > Everyone in the family shares in the care of the pets.
   > Every one of us has a favorite pet.

6. *maybe.* Possibly, perhaps.
   may be. A verb phrase suggesting something might or might not be.
   > Maybe we have too many pets, but is that even possible?
   > It may be that once the kids go to college, our parents will want even more pets.

TIP: *Awesome*, *cool*, and *totally* are three of the most frequently abused words in current English conversation. They are quickly losing any meaning because of their overuse. So try to substitute other, more precise words to convey your meaning.

WORDS THAT GET ABUSED

Here are some of the most frequently abused words—ones used incorrectly you can easily use correctly if you pay careful attention to their meanings.

1. *being that*. These words are incorrect when used as a phrase.
   Being that I love animals, I'm planning to become a vet. (incorrect usage)
   Being an animal lover, I plan to become a vet. (correct)
2. *hopeful*. An adjective that describes someone full of hope.
   hopefully. An adverb that means doing something with hope.
   I am hopeful that my grades will get me into vet school. (correct)
   Hopefully I'll do well in school. (incorrect)
   I am studying hopefully, and working as hard as I can. (correct)
3. *regardless*. Without taking into account. **Note:** there is no such word as *irregardless*.
   Irregardless of my grades, my experience with animals should help. (incorrect)
   Regardless of my grades, my experience with animals should help. (correct)
4. *like*. A preposition that introduces the idea of similarity
   as. An adverb that suggests similarity, or *in the same manner*
   A donkey's hee-haw is like an alarm clock; it startles and surprises you. (correct)
   Do like I say. (incorrect)
   Do as I say, not as I do. (correct)

TIP: Try to cut down dramatically on your use of the word *like*. It's probably the single most overused word. It's not a word to introduce sentences randomly, or to use when you can't think of what you're going to say next!

5. real. An adjective that describes something that is not false.
   really. An adverb that intensifies the verb it modifies. Do not use *real* when you mean *really*.

   > Keeping pets gives you a really good lesson in the nature of the real world. (correct)
   > My pet snake is real slithery and scares many people. (incorrect)
   > My pet snake is really slithery and scares many people. (correct)

6. *suppose*. To assume something is true, or to consider it as possible.
   supposed. The past tense of the verb *suppose*.

   > I suppose we learned from our parents how to love animals. (correct)
   > We are suppose to take care of them out of love, not obligation. (incorrect)
   > I am supposed to study harder if I am serious about becoming a vet. (correct)

TIP: Remember always to include the final *d* for the past tense of *suppose*. Too frequently, the word is used without the final *d*, and this immediately signals that the speaker either isn't well educated or doesn't care about language.

PRACTICE 1: USING CONFUSING WORDS CORRECTLY

Circle the correct word in each sentence.

1. Janet gave me a (compliment/complement) about my essay.

2. The class (all together/altogether) has seven iPods, five cell phones, and two iPhones.

3. Paul is always anxious to (adapt/adopt) every new technology as soon as it appears on the market.

4. The (continual/continuous) appearance of new cable channels makes TV watching both exciting and confusing.

5. (Everyone/Every one) of my favorite shows is on a different channel, so I'm constantly fingering the remote.

PRACTICE 2: REMEMBERING NOT TO ABUSE WORDS

Circle the correct word in each sentence.

1. The candidate and his staff counted (hopeful/hopefully) on volunteers to help get out the votes.

2. The Ironman triathlon race is (real, really) hard on the runners' endurance.

3. Lance Armstrong is a (real/really) hero to all bikers.

4. All athletes are (suppose/supposed) to train energetically, but some fail to do so.

5. Regardless of what the others suggest, do (as/like) I do, and you'll succeed.

Lesson 28 Words You Should Now Know

all together	hopeful
altogether	hopefully
as	like
complement	maybe
compliment	may be
continual	regardless
continuous	suppose
everyone	supposed
every one	

Extra Word(s) You Learned in This Lesson

_____

_____

_____

_____

ANSWERS

Practice 1: Using Confusing Words Correctly

1. compliment
2. all together
3. adopt
4. continual
5. Every one

Practice 2: Remembering Not to Abuse Words

1. hopefully
2. really
3. real
4. supposed
5. as

words about words

The finest words in the world are only vain
sounds if you cannot understand them.
ANATOLE FRANCE (1844–1924)
FRENCH AUTHOR AND NOVELIST

In this lesson, you'll focus on some interesting words about words. There are many, and they can help you become more precise, and more powerful, as a speaker and writer.

AS YOU'VE BECOME aware while reading this book, every profession and subject has words that are unique to it. You now know that philologists study languages, and etymology is the study of the how words developed over time. There's even a special name for the study of spelling—it's called orthography—and onomatologists study names. So it should come as no surprise that words themselves are a subject area.

The combined learning of all these specialized fields, along with the study of literature and poetry, has resulted in a long list of words about words. You'll learn some of them here, and you'll probably be surprised by how precisely they describe other words and how words are used. You'll also notice that many describe the ways in which you yourself speak and write.

TIP: Check your own speech and writing for some of the words in this lesson. For example, do you use superfluous words, clichés, circumlocutions, or non sequiturs?

WORDS ABOUT WORDS

1. *ambiguous.* A vague, unclear, or indefinite word, expression, sentence, or meaning. *Our teacher's instructions about how to write our essays were quite ambiguous, which confused us all.*

2. *analogy.* A comparison between two things that suggests that they show a similarity in at least some aspects. *Many people draw an analogy between how our brains work and how computers function.*

3. *circumlocution.* A roundabout or indirect way of speaking; the use of more words than necessary to express an idea. *My grandfather was famous in the family for his long-winded circumlocutions about what life was like when he was a boy.*

4. *cliché.* A trite, overused expression or idea that has lost its originality and impact. *Our school nurse was forever repeating her favorite timeworn cliché,* An apple a day keeps the doctor away.

5. *epigram/epigraph.* An epigram is a short, witty poem, saying, or quotation that conveys a single thought in a clever way. An epigraph is a brief quotation that appears at the beginning of an article, essay, or novel to introduce the theme. *Every lesson in this book has been introduced with an epigram used as an epigraph.*

6. *non sequitur.* A statement or conclusion that doesn't follow logically from what preceded it. *John's suggestion that we all protest the requirement of school uniforms was a non sequitur after the principal's announcement that our summer vacation was going to be cut short.*

7. *nuance.* A slight degree of difference in meaning, feeling, or tone of something spoken or written. *The poet's varied description of the joys of spring included subtle nuances that made us think of the changing seasons in an entirely new light.*

8. *redundant.* Speaking or writing that repeats the same idea several times. *In order to meet the requirement of 300 words, Jane filled her essay with many redundant sentences that added no new ideas to her topic.*

9. *rhetorical question.* A question asked with no expectation of a reply. *The teacher asked us, rhetorically, if we thought we should have more homework.*

10. *simile.* A statement using the words *like* or *as* to compare two dissimilar things. The valentine he sent me said *Your face is like a rose.* Similes are often confused with metaphors, which compare without using the words *like* and *as.* For example, a valentine might say, *You are my special rose.*

11. *superfluous.* Something that's unnecessary, or more than enough or required. *Reminding us to do our best on the final test is a superfluous bit of advice from our teacher.*

12. *verbiage.* An overabundance of words in writing or speech. *The doctor's verbiage confused me, but my mother was able to figure out what he meant.*

PRACTICE 1: MATCH WORDS ABOUT WORDS WITH THEIR MEANING

Draw lines to match each word about words with its meaning.

Word about Words
1. circumlocution
2. ambiguous
3. non sequitur
4. nuance
5. analogy
6. simile
7. cliché
8. epigram
9. superfluous
10. redundant

Meaning
a. a trite, overused expression
b. a comparison between two things that are mostly dissimilar
c. a short, witty statement that conveys an idea in a clever way
d. roundabout way of speaking
e. unnecessary or more than sufficient
f. using more words than necessary, repetitious
g. a slight shading of meaning
h. a vague or unclear word or statement
i. a comparison using the word *like* or *as*
j. a statement that does not follow logically

PRACTICE 2: WORDS ABOUT WORDS CROSSWORD PUZZLE

Across

1 comparison between two things or ideas

2 trite, overused expression

3 comparison using *like* or *as*

6 unnecessary, more than required

Down

1 vague, unclear

2 roundabout, indirect way of speaking

4 short, clever saying

5 repetitious (in speaking or writing)

Word Bank

ambiguous

analogy

circumlocution

cliché

epigram

redundant

simile

superfluous

Lesson 29 Words You Should Now Know

ambiguous	onomatologist
analogy	orthography
circumlocution	redundant
cliché	rhetorical question
epigram	simile
epigraph	superfluous
non sequitur	verbiage

Extra Word(s) You Learned in this Lesson

_____

_____

_____

_____

ANSWERS

Practice 1: Matching Words about Words with their Meaning

1. d
2. h
3. j
4. g
5. b
6. i
7. a
8. c
9. e
10. f

Practice 2: Words about Words Crossword Puzzle

Across	Down
1 analogy	**1** ambiguous
2 cliché	**2** circumlocution
3 simile	**4** epigram
6 superfluous	**5** redundant

words with extra power

> *Be simple in words, manners, and gestures. Amuse as well*
> *as instruct. If you can make a man laugh, you can make*
> *him think and make him like and believe you.*
> ALFRED. E. SMITH, JR. (1873–1944)
> NEW YORK GOVERNOR AND CANDIDATE FOR U.S. PRESIDENT

In this lesson, you'll learn some words that carry extra punch. They deliver a lot of meaning and power all by themselves.

CONGRATULATIONS ON REACHING the last lesson in the book! If you've read carefully, done the practice exercises, and remembered to use your new words in your everyday life, you've done a wonderful job of acquiring hundreds of new words.

By now, you've also gained an appreciation of how powerful words can be. They help you communicate ideas, thoughts, feelings, and opinions; they help you persuade, and they help you amuse. Words can also help you gain higher grades; compliments from teachers, parents, and friends; and an increased sense of confidence in your reading, writing, and speaking.

In this last lesson, you will find a list of words that are particularly powerful. They're noteworthy for their efficiency: they condense complicated thoughts into single words. Use these words when you want to avoid the circumlocutions and redundancies—those bad speaking and writing habits you learned about in the previous lesson. All the words in this lesson are adjectives, the most versatile part of speech. You might want to look back at Lesson 11 to review some other powerful adjectives you've learned. As you learn these new adjectives, stop to think about how many additional words it might take to convey the meaning of just one well-chosen adjective.

....

TIP: Words with extra power convey complicated meanings in a small space, an ideal goal for anyone seeking true vocabulary breadth and power.

....

WORDS WITH EXTRA POWER

1. *cacophonous.* Describes loud, confusing, and disagreeable sound or noise. *My parents consider my favorite hip hop music nothing but cacophonous noise.*
2. *demure.* Modest, reserved, and even shy. *Cinderella is a classic example of a demure young woman.*
3. *esoteric.* Understood by or meant for only the special few who have private or secret knowledge. *The study of prehistoric fish is quite an esoteric field, but one that is truly fascinating.*
4. *feminist.* Refers to the philosophy or political doctrine that holds that social, political, and all other rights of women should be equal to those of men. *The feminist movement has continued its struggle over the past 150 years to gain equal rights for women.*
5. *glib.* Said of speaking or writing that is fluent and smooth, but is also superficial and shows little preparation or sincere concern. *The candidate's glib responses to all the reporter's questions made me suspicious about her real qualifications for office.*
6. *ironic.* Seeking to communicate a meaning that is actually the opposite of its literal meaning; a contradiction between what is said and what is meant. *The story's title,* A Happy Ending, *was clearly ironic since almost all the characters were disappointed or dead by the end.*
7. *obsequious.* Acting submissive and flattering to someone perceived to be more powerful. *In my math class, there is one obsequious boy who is always trying to win favor with the teacher; he figures he can do less work if he becomes the teacher's pet.*

8. *ominous.* Threatening, or seeming to promise evil or harm. *Our teacher's ominous suggestion that we should get a good night's sleep before our next test scared us into studying harder.*

9. *pompous.* Puffed up with vanity and pretending to be grand and elegant. *The political candidate lost the race because of his huge promises and pompous speeches that voters felt were insincere.*

10. *sadistic.* Finding pleasure in being cruel. *Billy, our class bully, was feared because of his sadistic delight in making fun of weaker boys.*

11. *sardonic.* Ironically humorous; sarcastically mocking. *Homer Simpson is a sardonic husband, making fun of his wife and kids all the time.*

12. *sophisticated.* Worldly wise, educated, and experienced. *A student with a sophisticated vocabulary is assured easier essay writing as well as higher grades.*

PRACTICE 1: IDENTIFYING POWERFUL ADJECTIVES

Fill in each blank with the adjective from this lesson that fits the description. The first letter of each correct answer has been provided.

1. John always seems to speak easily and know what he is talking about. g_____

2. The band forgot to tune their instruments, and the result was a horrible kind of noise. c_____

3. Sally was determined to improve the rights of women, and believed in this set of beliefs. f_____

4. Billy was known for his cruelty and was often accused of enjoying insulting others. s_____

5. Jeremy was always trying too hard to please the people he wanted for friends. o_____

PRACTICE 2: WORDS WITH EXTRA POWER CROSSWORD PUZZLE

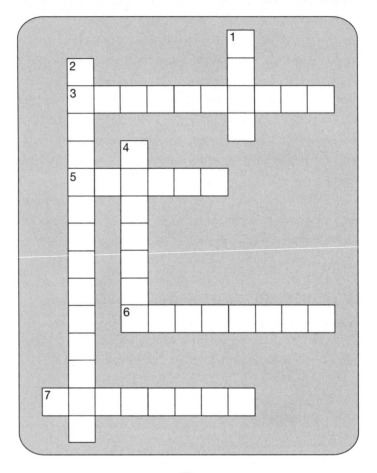

Across

3 always too willing to please

5 saying the opposite of what is meant

6 enjoys being cruel

7 belief in women's rights

Down

1 speaks fluently and maybe too easily

2 educated, worldly wise

4 speaks with false grandness

Word Bank

feminist

glib

ironic

obsequious

pompous

sadistic

sophisticated

Lesson 30 Words You Should Now Know

cacophonous	obsequious
demure	ominous
esoteric	pompous
feminist	sadistic
glib	sardonic
ironic	sophisticated

Extra Word(s) You Learned in This Lesson

_____

_____

_____

_____

ANSWERS

Practice 1: Identifying Powerful Adjectives

1. glib
2. cacophonous
3. feminist
4. sadistic
5. obsequious

Practice 2: Words with Extra Power Crossword Puzzle

Across
3 obsequious
5 ironic
6 sadistic
7 feminist

Down
1 glib
2 sophisticated
4 pompous

P O S T T E S T

NOW THAT YOU'VE completed all the lessons in the book, take this 30-question posttest. It's similar to the pretest you took before beginning the lessons, except the questions are different this time.

This posttest lets you measure how your word power has improved. After completing the test and evaluating your score, you may want to go back and revisit some practice exercises. Alternatively, reviewing the vocabulary words in the book's glossary is another useful strategy for refreshing your knowledge.

The test should take about 30 minutes to complete. The answer key at the end of the test provides the lesson number in which each question's vocabulary word appears. Don't peek, and good luck!

1. A *synonym* is
    a. a law that protects animals.
    b. a word that means the opposite.
    c. a word that means the same.
    d. a law that covers financial matters.

2. An *antonym* is
    a. an apology offered formally.
    b. a person who fights for the other side.
    c. a word borrowed from Latin or Greek.
    d. a word that means the opposite.

3. The best place to look up a word's meaning is
    a. a good dictionary.
    b. a thesaurus.
    c. the index of a book.
    d. Wikipedia.

4. The word *nuance* means
    a. the first definition of a word.
    b. the strict dictionary definition of a word.
    c. the subtle differences in meanings of words.
    d. the word suggestions in a thesaurus.

5. The word *denotation* means
    a. the ending of a word.
    b. the main part of a word.
    c. the strict dictionary definition of a word.
    d. the origin of a word.

6. The word *connotation* means
    a. the emotional or cultural meaning of a word.
    b. the strict dictionary definition of a word.
    c. the substitution of one word for another.
    d. the idea that is the word's starting point.

7. The word *antecedent* describes
  a. something that doesn't move.
  b. something that comes before.
  c. something that is ancient.
  d. something that is controversial.

8. To *synchronize* is to
  a. make something happen very quickly.
  b. suggest an alternative idea.
  c. make something happen at the same time.
  d. ask an irrelevant question.

9. A *pseudonym* is
  a. a false name.
  b. an ancient god or deity.
  c. a harsh sound.
  d. an evil opponent.

10. To *fluctuate* is to
  a. fly at very high altitudes.
  b. flutter in the breeze.
  c. change frequently.
  d. feel sickly and nauseous.

11. The opposite of the word *inevitable* is
  a. certain to happen.
  b. may never happen.
  c. likely to happen.
  d. out of reach.

12. When you have an *incentive*, you have a
  a. reason to stop doing something.
  b. an extra part of something that can easily be separated.
  c. the last item in a list or series.
  d. a stimulus to complete a task.

13. To give someone *clemency* is to give them

    a. a stiff sentence for a crime committed.

    b. a gift of enormous value.

    c. mercy and forgiveness.

    d. the right to manage on their own.

14. *Mediation* is

    a. intervention to settle a disagreement.

    b. finding the middle ground.

    c. granting someone forgiveness.

    d. supporting the opposing viewpoint.

15. *Amnesty* is

    a. a choice between two alternatives.

    b. safety from punishment or prosecution.

    c. the right to have a lawyer represent you.

    d. a state of calm, with no disturbances.

16. To *augment* is to

    a. listen to an opposing argument.

    b. consider changing positions.

    c. to increase or add to something.

    d. to accomplish or achieve something.

17. To *allocate* is to

    a. increase the size of something.

    b. decrease the size of something.

    c. improve the condition of something.

    d. set something aside for a special purpose.

18. To *compile* is to

    a. put together from various sources.

    b. criticize an idea or position.

    c. reach an accurate conclusion.

    d. reach a false conclusion.

19. To *interpret* is to
   a. gather ideas together.
   b. explain or translate from one form to another.
   c. use an illogical argument.
   d. understand something correctly.

20. To be *pretentious* is to
   a. try to impress others.
   b. be very wise.
   c. be confident.
   d. be afraid to speak up.

21. Being *elated* means
   a. being dejected and unhappy.
   b. being satisfied.
   c. being willing to try anything.
   d. being delighted and pleased.

22. Being *humiliated* means
   a. being thrilled and happy.
   b. being disappointed.
   c. being frustrated.
   d. being embarrassed and looked down on.

23. *Genealogy* is the study of
   a. prehistoric animals.
   b. family histories.
   c. the pharaohs of Egypt.
   d. the development of plants.

24. To send *condolences* is to
   a. send sympathy to someone grieving.
   b. send regrets to an invitation.
   c. send formal invitations to a wedding.
   d. send a formal letter of application.

25. *Euphemisms* are
   a. formal invitations to events.
   b. synonyms for other words.
   c. substitutions of milder words for unpleasant ones.
   d. formal birth announcements.

26. The meaning of *copyright* is that
   a. anyone is free to copy material they see in print.
   b. no one is free to copy material they see in print.
   c. everything on the Internet is free to use.
   d. the author alone may grant the right to copy material.

27. To *implement* a plan is
   a. to investigate solutions to a problem.
   b. to find the answer to a problem.
   c. to put the plan in action.
   d. to change the steps to be taken in the plan.

28. A *caucus* is
   a. a new idea introduced to a process.
   b. a complicated solution to a problem.
   c. a meeting in support of a particular interest.
   d. a new set of ideas or beliefs.

29. A *feminist* is
   a. a very intelligent woman.
   b. a professional woman in a corporation.
   c. a person who believes in equal rights for women.
   d. a female anthropologist.

30. Someone who is *sadistic*
   a. likes to tease and tell jokes.
   b. is a grieving person.
   c. is a person who often misrepresents truth.
   d. is a person who enjoys being cruel.

ANSWERS

1. c (Lesson 1)
2. d (Lesson 1)
3. a (Lesson 2)
4. c (Lesson 2)
5. c (Lesson 4)
6. a (Lesson 4)
7. b (Lesson 6)
8. c (Lesson 6)
9. a (Lesson 6)
10. c (Lesson 8)
11. b (Lesson 8)
12. d (Lesson 8)
13. c (Lesson 10)
14. a (Lesson 10)
15. b (Lesson 10)
16. c (Lesson 12)
17. d (Lesson 12)
18. a (Lesson 12)
19. b (Lesson 12)
20. a (Lesson 14)
21. d (Lesson 15)
22. d (Lesson 15)
23. b (Lesson 20)
24. a (Lesson 21)
25. c (Lesson 21)
26. d (Lesson 25)
27. c (Lesson 24)
28. c (Lesson 24)
29. c (Lesson 30)
30. d (Lesson 30)

hints for taking standardized tests

THE TERM *standardized test* has the ability to produce fear in test takers. These tests are often given by a state board of education or a nationally recognized education group. Usually these tests are taken in the hope of getting accepted—whether it's for a special program, the next grade in school, or even to a college or university. Here's the good news: standardized tests are more familiar to you than you know. In most cases, these tests look very similar to tests that your teachers may have given in the classroom.

The following pages include valuable tips for combating test anxiety—that sinking or blank feeling some people feel as they begin a test or encounter a difficult question. You'll discover how to use your time wisely and how to avoid errors when you're taking a test. Also, you will find a plan for preparing for the test and for the test day. Once you have these tips down, you're ready to approach any exam head-on!

COMBATING TEST ANXIETY

Take the Test One Question at a Time

Focus all your attention on the question you're answering. Block out any thoughts about questions you've already read or concerns about what's coming next. Concentrate your thinking where it will do the most good—on the present question.

If You Lose Your Concentration

Don't worry about it! It's normal. During a long test, it happens to everyone. When your mind is stressed, it takes a break whether you want it to or not. It's easy to get your concentration back if you simply acknowledge the fact that you've lost it and take a quick break.

If You Freeze Before or During the Test

Don't worry about a question that stumps you. Mark it and go on to the next question. You can come back to the "stumper" later. Try to put it out of your mind completely until you come back to it. Chances are, the memory block will be gone by the time you return to the question.

If you freeze before you even begin the test, here's what to do:

1. Take a little time to look over the test.
2. Read a few of the questions.
3. Decide which are the easiest and start there.
4. Before long, you'll be "in the groove."

TIME STRATEGIES

With the strategies in this section, you'll notice the next timed test you take is not as scary.

Pace Yourself

The most important time strategy is pacing yourself. Before you begin, take just a few seconds to survey the test, noting the number of questions and the sections that look easier than the rest. Estimate a time schedule based upon the amount of time available to you. Mark the halfway point on your test and make a note beside that mark of what the time will be when the testing period is half over.

Keep Moving

Once you begin the test, keep moving. If you work slowly in an attempt to make fewer mistakes, your mind will become bored and begin to wander, and you will lose concentration.

The Process of Elimination

For some standardized tests, there is no guessing penalty. What this means is that you shouldn't be afraid to guess. For a multiple-choice question with four answer choices, you have a one in four chance of guessing correctly. And your chances improve if you can eliminate a choice or two.

By using the process of elimination, you will cross out incorrect answer choices and improve your odds of finding the correct answer. In order for the process of elimination to work, you must keep track of what choices you are crossing out. Cross out incorrect choices on the test booklet itself. If you don't cross out an incorrect answer, you may still think it is a possible answer. Crossing out any incorrect answers makes it easier to identify the right answer: There will be fewer places where it can hide!

AVOIDING ERRORS

When you take a test, you want to make as few errors as possible in the questions you answer. Following are a few tactics to keep in mind.

Control Yourself

If you feel rushed or worried, stop for a few seconds. Acknowledging the feeling (*Hmmm! I'm feeling a little pressure here!*), take a few deep breaths, and send yourself a few positive messages (*I am prepared for this test, and I will do well!*).

Directions

In many standardized testing situations, specific instructions are given and you must follow them as best as you can. Be sure you understand what is expected. If you don't, ask. Listen carefully for instructions about how to answer the questions and make certain you know how much time you have to complete the task. If you miss any important information about the rules of taking the test, **ask for it**.

If You Finish Early

Use any time you have left at the end of the test or test section to check your work. First, make sure you've put the right answers in the right places. After you've checked for errors, take a second look at the more difficult questions. If you have a good reason for thinking your first response was wrong, change it.

THE DAYS BEFORE THE TEST

Physical Activity

Get some exercise in the days preceding the test. Play a game outside with your friends or take your pet for a walk. Exercise helps give more oxygen to your brain and allows your thinking performance to rise on the day you take the test. But moderation is key here. You don't want to exercise so much that you feel too tired; however, a little physical activity will do the trick.

Balanced Diet

Like your body, your brain needs the proper nutrients to function well. Eat plenty of fruits and vegetables in the days before the test. Foods like fish and beans are also good choices to help your mind reach its best level of performance before a big test.

Rest

Get plenty of sleep the nights before the test. Go to bed at a reasonable time, and you'll feel relaxed and rested.

TEST DAY

It's finally here: the day of the big test! Eat a good breakfast, and avoid anything high in sugar (even though it might taste good, no sugary cereal or doughnuts). If you can, get to your classroom early so you can review your materials before the test begins. The best thing to do next is to relax and think positively! Before you know it, the test will be over, and you'll walk away knowing you did your absolute best!

GLOSSARY

accept   recognize or take on something

acronym   pronounceable word formed from the initial letters or syllables of a series of words

acrophobia   fear of heights

adapt   to adjust or modify something

ad hoc   (from Latin for *for this*) created right now, or improvised, for a specific purpose

ad hominem   (from Latin for *to the man*) argument that attacks someone's character rather than facts by appealing to the emotions rather than the intellect

adjacent   bordering on, being next to, or close, or neighboring

adopt   to accept as one's own

advocate   a person who argues on behalf of an idea or another person

aerobic   something or someone that utilizes oxygen in order to live

affect   to modify or change something

agoraphobia   an abnormal fear of open spaces, crowds, and public areas

agrarian   relating to the cultivation of the land or farming

all ready   the state of being prepared for something

all together   a group of things or persons gathered together

all ways   every method or path available

allocate   to set aside for a specific purpose

already   by this time

altogether   entirely, completely

altruistic   unselfishly interested in the welfare of others

always   forever, as in time

ambiguous   unclear, unspecific, open to interpretation

amiable   friendly, good-natured, comfortable with others

amnesia   in extreme cases, the total loss of memory

amnesty   the granting of a pardon, or immunity for an offense, by a head of state

anachronism   something that is out of order chronologically or belongs to another time

analogy   a comparison between two things that suggests that they are similar in at least some aspects

analogous   similar in at least some aspects

ancestor   a person from whom one is descended, especially if more remote than a grandparent

anime   (from the Japanese word for *animation*) animation done in the Japanese style

antecedent   something that comes before something else, preceding another

anthropology   the study of the origins, customs, beliefs, and social relationships of groups of human beings

antonym   a word that has the opposite meaning of another word

apathetic   lazy, uninterested, indifferent

arachnophobia   an extreme fear of spiders

arbiter   a person appointed to settle differences between two individuals or groups

archive   a place for storing acquired information, often historical material

artistic   having creative skills or a serious interest in the arts

as   adverb that suggests similarity, or *in the same manner*

astronomy   the study of outer space, especially the examination of all material objects and phenomena outside Earth's atmosphere

attain   to accomplish or achieve

audiologist   a medical specialist in the study and treatment of hearing, especially hearing defects

augment   to increase or add to

autonomy   self-government or independence

BFF   abbreviation of *best friend forever*

bibliography   a list of books or other documents consulted in the creation of a written work

biography   the story of someone's life

biology   the study of all living organisms

botany   the study of plants

breath   the intake of air

breathe   the process of using the air

browser   someone who explores at random, as in a library; in computer terms, a program that is used to view, download, surf, or otherwise view pages on the Internet

cacophonous   loud, confusing, and disagreeable sound or noise

calisthenics   gymnastic exercises that are usually performed with little or no special apparatus

camouflage   (from the French for *to disguise*) disguising something to fool an enemy, particularly the painting of clothing to resemble the surrounding countryside of a battle

capital   the most important city in a country; or in general, the biggest or most important; or in financial terms, money or wealth

capitol   the building that houses the government in a capital city

cardiology   the branch of medicine that addresses the diagnosis and treatment of disorders of the heart

caucus   a meeting organized in support of a particular interest, group, or cause

caveat emptor   (from the Latin for *let the buyer beware*) the concept that buyers are responsible for judging the quality of what they buy; the seller is not necessarily to be trusted

cease   to stop or end a process

cell-phone manners   the set of appropriate customs for conducting cell-phone conversations

cerebral   relating to the brain, or the intellect as opposed to the emotions

cessation   an end or stop to something

challenge   an invitation to competition or to achieve a new standard

chaotic   very disorganized and without clear purpose

chronic   continuous over a long time

chronicle   a written account of events, usually in chronological order

chronology   the order in which things occur in time

circumlocution   a roundabout or indirect way of speaking; the use of more words than necessary to express an idea

claustrophobia   fear of small spaces, such as elevators or closets

clemency   forgiveness or decreasing of a punishment assigned

cliché   a trite, overused expression or idea that has lost its originality and impact.

cocoa   (from the Spanish name for the bean of the cacao tree) the chocolate beverage made from the powder ground from roasted cacao beans

coherent   a part of an organized whole; sticking together

collateral damage   euphemism for killing innocent bystanders

communicate   to give information

compensate   to pay someone; to make up for something else

compile   to put together from various sources

complacent   self-satisfied; confident in his or her opinions

complement   something that is added in, that contributes

compliment   a remark that pleases or flatters someone

component   a small part of a larger whole

concede   to give in to; to yield to another's position

concurrent   happening at the same time

condolences   the expression of sympathy with a person who is suffering sorrow, misfortune, or grief

connotation   a meaning that is suggested or implied, but not directly stated

consensus   general agreement among members of a group or community

consequence   the result of something; that which follows something that came before

constituent   a part of a whole; also, a resident of a place represented by an elected official

contempt   the feeling of finding someone or something inferior or not worthy of respect; also, the state of being thought inferior or disgraced

context   the text surrounding a word that provides clues to the word's meaning

continual   happening repeatedly, over and over again

continuous   occurring without interruption

controversial   a position or argument that prompts debate

copyright law   the law that grants to the author (or other owner of the copyright) the exclusive right to make copies or allow others to make copies of anything created or written, including literary, musical, artistic, audio, and video works

Craigslist   a network of local communities, featuring (mostly) free classified advertisements in a variety of categories

decathlon   an athletic contest comprising ten different track-and-field events and won by the contestant amassing the highest total score

decipher   to read a code or text that is illegible or difficult to understand

deduce   to reach a conclusion using logic or facts

dejected   sad, disappointed, pessimistic

delirious   feeling uncontrolled excitement or happiness

demanding   requiring strength or patience

demure   modest, reserved, and even shy

denotation   the result; stating something clearly and precisely

deposition   a statement of evidence or factual information

derive   to receive or understand something from something or somewhere else

dermatologist   a specialist in the branch of medicine dealing with the skin and its diseases

descendant   a person, animal, or plant descended from a specific ancestor

desktop publishing   the use of computer software that enables the design and production of professional-looking publications on a home computer

despise   to look at something or someone with contempt, hatred, or disgust

devour   eat quickly, hungrily

diagnostic   a technique for finding the root or cause

dilemma   a situation in which a choice must be made between two options

diminish   to make smaller or less important

discipline   field of knowledge

disinterested   having no opinion either way; having no selfish motive

distort   to bring something out of shape; to misrepresent the facts

docile   easily controlled or supervised; meek and mild

dogma   a principle or belief thought to be absolutely true

domain name   an internet address owned by a person or organization to identify the location of its Web pages; domain suffixes indicate the type of material on the pages at that address

draft   in sports, the selection by a professional team of new players from a group of amateur players

dual   two, or double of something

dubious   uncertain; unclear; not obviously one thing or another

duel   a formal fight between opposing parties

dynasty   a sequence of rulers from the same family, as in the Ming Dynasty of Chinese history; also, a family group notable for a particular quality, such as wealth

eclectic   derived from a mixture or selected from various sources

ecstatic   extraordinarily joyous; being in a state of ecstasy

effect   the result of something

egotist   a person who is self-centered, and thinks he is better or more interesting than others

elated   delighted, pleased; slightly less joyful than ecstatic, but showing great happiness

eloquent   persuasive and easily communicating or defending a position

empathy   the ability to understand or sympathize with another's point of view

empirical   based on experience; established by observation or physical fact

energetically   doing something with notable energy, dedication, or extra effort

English Language Learners   people learning English as a second language

enhance   to improve something, or make it greater

enigma   a problem or statement that is mysterious, or difficult to understand

enormous   extremely large

ensure   to make something or some idea certain

enthusiastically   doing something with eagerness or intensity of feeling

entomology   the study of insects

envy   to feel discontent about another's possessions or qualities

epigram   a short, witty poem saying, or quotation that conveys a single thought in a clever way

epigraph   a brief quotation that appears at the beginning of articles, essays, or novels to introduce the theme of the narrative that follows

esoteric   understood by or meant for only the special few who have private or secret knowledge

etiquette   the unwritten rules governing socially acceptable behavior and defining good manners

etymologist   someone who studies the origins and development of words

etymology   the study of the origins and historical development of words, including the changes that occur in words as they move from one language to another

euphemism   a mild, indirect, or vague expression substituted for one thought to be offensive, harsh, or blunt.

every one   the specific individuals in a group

everyone   a pronoun that describes a group; everybody in the group

exceed   to be larger or greater than something else

except   to exclude something

executive   an officer or administrator in an organization who supervises others

exorbitant   an extravagant, excessive amount or quality

experimentally   doing something in a careful way, following established procedures to establish the truth of something

expertly   doing something with an extraordinary amount of skill and knowledge

explicit   clear, precise, detailed

extremely   doing something at the furthest reach, or at a level distant from the norm

extrovert   an outgoing, gregarious person who enjoys the company of others

facilitate   to make something happen more easily

family tree   a genealogical chart showing the ancestry, descent, and relationship of all members of a family or other genealogical group

fascinating   to have interesting qualities or characteristics

faux pas   (from the French for *false step*) an embarrassing mistake in manners or conduct

federal   referring to the central government of a country that consists of several states

feminist   one who espouses the philosophy or political doctrine that social, political, and all other rights of women should be equal to those of men

finite   limited, with boundaries; not eternal

flag display   the laws that govern the display of the U.S. flag

fluctuate   to swing or move back and forth irregularly

fluency   ease or ability to speak, read, or understand in a language

frantically   doing something in a rush or in panic

fraud   a deceptive act with the intent of making an unfair financial gain

friendly fire   euphemism for accidental killing of one's own comrades in war

frustrated   disappointed or unhappy because one is unable to achieve some goal or fulfill a desire

furious   full of fury, violent passion, or rage; also, full of energy or speed, as in a furious storm

futile   not worth the effort; doomed to failure

genealogy   a record of the descent of a person, family, or group from an ancestor or ancestors; also, the study of family histories

generation   generally, the entire number of people born and living at about the same time; technically, the period of 30 years, accepted as the average period between the birth of parents and the birth of their offspring

genuine   not false or modified; real and natural

geocaching   a type of treasure hunt for caches (boxes), which usually contain a logbook in which players record their names

geology   the study of the physical history of Earth and its rocks

glib   superficial, fluent, and smooth; showing little preparation or sincere concern

gluttonous   given to overindulgence, especially in food

gourmet   a person who is very serious about the quality of food; sometimes called a foodie

grasp   to grip something physically; to understand something

grueling   extremely difficult or exhausting

hierarchy   the arrangement of anything, usually people, in order of rank or importance

holding back   failing a student for a whole grade year

homonym   a word that is pronounced the same as another word but is different in spelling and meaning

homophone   one of two or more words pronounced alike but different in meaning or spelling

hopeful   adjective that describes someone full of hope

hopefully   adverb that means doing something with hope

horrified   stricken with horror; intensely fearful or revolted by something or someone

hostel   an inexpensive lodging place for overnight stays

humiliated   strongly embarrassed by a loss of respect or admiration from others

hypochondria   excessive concern or talk about one's health, often with concentration on a particular form of illness

icon   a picture or image that stands for something else; in computer terms, a picture or symbol that represents a command or an available program or function

ideology   a set of ideas or beliefs that form the basis of a political, economic, or philosophical system

implement   a tool; or to bring something about, to make something happen. As a noun, this word describes an instrument or tool used to perform some activity. As a verb, it describes the act of performing an activity, or making something happen.

implicit   suggested, implied, or understood but not directly stated

imply   to say something indirectly, in a suggestive manner

inadequate   not sufficient, not adequate, not enough

incentive   something, often a reward of money, that motivates or encourages someone to do something

incorporate   add to something else

inevitable   something that is impossible to prevent or stop

infrastructure   the basic foundation or facilities and services needed for the functioning of a community or a system

inherent   a natural part of something that cannot be separated from it

innovationa new development

insomnia   inability to sleep

insure   to make something certain in financial terms

internist   a medical specialist in the diagnosis and nonsurgical treatment of diseases, especially of adults

interpret   to explain or to translate from one form into another

intimidate   to make someone timid or fearful; to exert control over others

intrinsic   basic to the nature of something or someone

introductions   the formal presentation of one person to another or others

introvert   a person who is shy and most comfortable with his or her own thoughts and feelings

ironic   seeking to communicate a meaning that is actually the opposite of what is meant literally

Ironman   annual triathlon race including an ocean swim, a bike ride, and a marathon foot race

ISP (Internet service provider)   a company or organization that provides access to the Internet, usually for a fee

italicize   to change the appearance of typed material in order to emphasize its importance

jealous   feeling resentful toward another because of that person's success or qualities or possessions

kickoff   in football and soccer, a kick that puts a stationary ball in motion and begins a period of play

kin a group of persons descended from a common ancestor or constituting a family, clan, tribe, or race

kinfolk another collective term for relatives

kinetic produced by motion

kleptomania a compulsion to steal, even without need or any specific desire

laconic using as few words as possible to communicate ideas

legible easily read

legislate to pass laws or modify existing laws

like a preposition that introduces the idea of similarity

linguist a person who speaks several languages fluently

lonely unhappy because of lack of presence of other people

loner a person who prefers to be alone, and avoids the company of others

loquacious very chatty, talkative

lucid clear and easily understandable

magical enchanting, charming, not of this world

manga the Japanese word for *comic books*

manners the socially acceptable way of acting, including all the approved customs of social interaction

marathon a long-distance running event of 26 miles and 385 yards

matinee (from the French for *morning*) an entertainment or performance held in the afternoon

may be a verb phrase suggesting something might or might not be

maybe possibly, perhaps

mediate to resolve differences or to bring about a settlement between conflicting parties

mediation an attempt by a third party to resolve differences between two parties

megalomania an obsession with grandiose or extravagant things or actions

melancholy extremely sad and depressed, often on an ongoing basis

mercy compassion toward those less fortunate

metaphor a word or phrase used to describe similarity between two things without using *like* or *as*

metamorphosis   a transformation or major change

mnemonic   a device or system designed to help remember something

monogamy   marriage with only one person at a time

multifaceted   having many sides or many aspects

multitasking   the common practice of doing more than one thing at a time

naïve   simple or innocent; lacking in experience or wisdom

narcissist   a person who thinks only of himself or herself

nemesis   an opponent or problem that cannot be overcome

netiquette   the rules of etiquette, or good manners, that have come to be acceptable during Internet communications

neurology   the branch of medicine that addresses the diagnosis and treatment of disorders of nerves and the nervous system

ninja   a person trained primarily in the Japanese martial art of ninjutsu

No Child Left Behind   the policy of testing student and school performance against national standards

non sequitur   a statement or conclusion that does not follow logically from what preceded it

nuance   a slight degree of difference in meaning, feeling, or tone in something spoken or written

nuclear family   a family unit consisting of a mother and a father and their children

nurse practitioner   a registered nurse (one who has earned a college-level RN degree) with advanced training who is qualified to perform some of the duties of a physician

objet d'art   (from the French for *object of art*) a work of art, usually small; sometimes simply called *objet* or (plural) *objets*

obsequious   acting submissive and flattering to someone perceived to be more powerful

obsessed   having intense or excessive interest in or concern for something or someone

obsession   an irrational devotion to an idea, opinion, or other person

obstetrician   a medical specialist who cares for women during pregnancy, childbirth, and the recuperative period following delivery

obvious   easily understood or observed

offsides   in football or soccer, illegally beyond an allowed line or area or ahead of the ball

ominous   threatening; seeming to promise evil or harm

oncologist   a medical specialist in the study of cancer, including tumor development, diagnosis, treatment, and prevention

onomatologist   a person who studies names

ophthalmologist   medical specialist who cares for the eye and its diseases

optometrist   a medical specialist who examines, diagnoses, and directs patients in the use of corrective vision lenses

organic   an adjective describing things developed from living organisms, or plants and animals raised without the use of drugs, hormones, or synthetic chemicals

orient   to find one's way, usually with a compass

ornithology   the branch of zoology that studies birds

orthodontist   a dental specialist whose task is the correction of irregularly aligned teeth, usually involving braces and sometimes oral surgery

orthography   the study of spelling

osteopath   a medical specialist who provides traditional medical treatments in the manipulation of muscles and bones

out of left field   unexpected or strange behavior

pacification   euphemism for killing or controlling citizens of enemy states

paleontology   the study of the life forms of prehistoric times, especially the fossils of plants, animals, and other organisms

paranoia   extreme, irrational distrust of others

patriotic   loving one's country; often associated with unselfish sacrifice

pediatrician   a medical specialist concerned with the development, care, and diseases of infants and children

pedigree   an ancestral line of descent or ancestry; in the animal world, a record of an animal's ancestry

perceive   to see or understand something that is difficult to understand

persecute   to punish in an extreme manner

persist   to continue to do something or to continue to happen

personal   belonging to an individual

personnel   all the employees in a company

petrified   so frightened that one is unable to move

phenomena   noteworthy events or facts (note: the singular form of the word is *phenomenon*)

philanthropy   the love of humankind; extending efforts to help others

philology   the scientific study of languages, including their historical development and the relationships between various languages

phobia   intense, often irrational feeling, especially fear of certain things

pirouette   (from the French for *spinning top*) in ballet, a complete turn of the body on the point of the toe or the ball of the foot

pizza   (from the Italian for *bite*) an open-faced baked pie topped usually with spiced tomato sauce, cheese, and other garnishes

placecards   small cards used with formal table settings to indicate where each guest is to sit

podiatrist   a medical specialist in the care, diagnosis, and treatment of disorders of the feet

policy   a course of action of an organization or government

polygamy   the practice of having more than one spouse (usually more than one wife) at one time; also called plural marriage

pompous   puffed up with vanity; pretending to be grand and elegant

post-traumatic stress disorder (PTSD)   emotional and mental disturbances resulting from war experiences

potpourri   (from the French for *rotten pot*) a mixture of dried flower petals and spices, kept in a jar for their fragrance; also, any mixture of assorted objects

precede   to go ahead of or before someone or something chronologically

predominant   the most common or important; the most dominant

prejudiced   holding an opinion formed without consideration of the facts; creating a negative impact on someone else

preliminary   happening before something else that is more important

pretentious   always trying to impress others; pretending to be very important or very wise

principal   the head of a school

principle   a doctrine or assumption

prioritize   to arrange or do in order of importance

pro bono publico   (from the Latin *for the public good*) something that is done without pay, for the public good; often shortened to *pro bono*

procedure   a way of performing a task; a series of steps to be followed

proceed   to move forward; to advance or continue in an established direction

prodigy   an unusually talented or gifted person, usually young

prosecute   to take legal action against someone

protocol   the customs, regulations, and etiquette that govern a particular situation; also, a document or treaty between states

prudent   cautious and practical in making difficult decisions

pseudonym   a false name, often used by writers to mask their identity

psychology   the scientific study of human and animal behavior

pyromania   an uncontrollable desire to set fires

quiescent   still, restful, quiet

rare   not often found; unusual

real   adjective that describes something that is not false

really   adverb that intensifies the verb it modifies

reconcile   to bring back together; to reestablish a relationship

redundant   repetitious, using more words than necessary to express an idea

referendum   a popular vote on a proposed law

regardless   without taking into account (note that there is no such word as *irregardless*)

reluctant   hesitant or uncertain about something

respect   the core word on which all etiquette systems are built

rhetorical question   a question asked solely for effect, with no expectation of a reply

road rage   aggressive and sometimes violent behavior by drivers annoyed by other drivers' behavior

RSVP   the initials of a French phrase, *répondez, s'il vous plaît* (*please reply*) typically used on formal invitations to indicate that the guest must respond, usually in writing, accepting or declining the invitation

sadistic   finding pleasure in being cruel

sadly   doing something out of unhappiness, or distress, or regret

sardonic   ironically humorous; sarcastically mocking

search engine   computer software that searches the Internet for documents that contain a keyword, phrase, or subject submitted by the user

serenity   a state of calmness, without disturbance

shout-out   an acknowledgment or greeting given for someone during a radio or television show, often used by rap musicians to acknowledge fans or mentors

sibling   one of two or more individuals having one common parent; a brother or sister

simile   a statement using the words *like* or *as* in comparing two things that are in most other ways dissimilar

social networking   websites that enable people to meet and share information

social promotion   euphemism for advancing a failing student to the next grade in spite of inadequate academic performance

sophisticated   worldly-wise; educated and experienced

spam   an unrequested commercial message on the Internet, usually sent as an email

special ed   education for students who have difficulty in regular classes

speed dating   a matchmaking process in which people seeking romantic partners meet others for brief (7 or 8 minutes) conversations before moving on to meet another participant

spokesman   one who speaks for a group

stationary   not moving; stable

stationery   writing materials, usually paper

streaming   is to flow, as in a river or a pitcher pouring a liquid; in computer terms, the technology that enables the delivery to your computer of a steady stream of information or images, such as a streaming video of a live concert

strive   to work to achieve a result; to continue with an effort

subjugate   to conquer or bring someone or something under control

subordinate   to make something less important; to be under someone's authority

subtle   not easy to grasp; describing something whose meaning is not obvious

successfully   doing something that achieves a goal; reaching success

suddenly doing something in a quick, unexpected way

sudoku a numbers puzzle in which the player is challenged to fill numbers into a grid of nine squares

superfluous unnecessary; more than sufficient or required

suppose to assume something is true, or to consider it as possible

supposed the past tense of the verb *suppose*

swiftly doing something quickly

synchronize to make two events happen at once

synonym a word that means the same as, or very close to, another word

taboo unacceptable, forbidden in polite society

technical a description of specific or useful information in a particular subject area

terrified seriously frightened or filled with terror

texting sending text messages via cell phones or other mobile devices

thank-you note a formal letter or a short note of thanks for hospitality or a gift

their refers to something belonging to them

there refers to a place where something is

thesaurus a publication that provides synonyms (and sometimes antonyms) for the words of a given language

they're contraction of *they are*

thoughtfully doing something with care and deliberation, or with dedicated thought

three strikes in baseball, a batter strikes out when he has struck at or failed to hit three good balls; in the law, the demand for specific, severe punishments (such as life imprisonment) after conviction for three felonies

time-out in sports, a brief interruption in play called so that the players may rest, deliberate, or make substitutions

timid exhibiting a lack of confidence; extremely shy and careful

unanimous in complete agreement; sharing the same position

underestimate to make too low an evaluation of value

uninterested not interested

uproarious noisy and uncontrolled, as laughter

URL (Uniform Resource Locator)   the system used for specifying addresses on the Internet; each individual file or page has its own URL, located on the address bar at the top of the Internet browser window

utilize   to make use of

verbiage   an overabundance of words in writing or speech

vertigo   a sensation of dizziness or spinning, even when standing or sitting on solid ground

versatile   useful in many ways

vigorously   doing something with energy and strength

vindictive   feeling anger combined with a strong desire for revenge

weather   the conditions in the climate

whether   conjunction meaning *or* or *perhaps*

who   pronoun for he, she, or they

whom   pronoun for him, her, or them

World Wide Web   the complete set of electronic documents that are connected over the Internet through use of the Hypertext Transfer Protocol (HTTP) for transferring data

your   refers to something that belongs to you

you're   contraction of *you are*

zoology   the study of animals